Probabilistic Risk Assessment Methods and Case Studies

July 25, 2014

Disclaimer

This document has been reviewed in accordance with U.S. Environmental Protection Agency (EPA) policy and approved for publication. Mention of trade names or commercial products does not constitute endorsement or recommendation for use.

This document was produced by a Technical Panel of the EPA Risk Assessment Forum (RAF). The authors drew on their experience in doing probabilistic assessments and interpreting them to improve risk management of environmental and health hazards. Interviews, presentations and dialogues with risk managers conducted by the Technical Panel have contributed to the insights and recommendations in this white paper and the associated document titled *Probabilistic Risk Assessment to Inform Decision Making: Frequently Asked Questions.*

Foreword

Throughout many of the U.S. Environmental Protection Agency's (EPA) program offices and regions, various forms of probabilistic methods have been used to answer questions about exposure and risk to humans, other organisms and the environment. Risk assessors, risk managers and others, particularly within the scientific and research divisions, have recognized that more sophisticated statistical and mathematical approaches could be utilized to enhance the quality and accuracy of Agency risk assessments. Various stakeholders, inside and outside of the Agency, have called for a more comprehensive characterization of risks, including uncertainties, to improve the protection of sensitive or vulnerable populations and lifestages.

The EPA identified the need to examine the use of probabilistic approaches in Agency risk assessments and decisions. The RAF developed this paper and the companion document, *Probabilistic Risk Assessment to Inform Decision Making: Frequently Asked Questions,* to provide a general overview of the value of probabilistic analyses and similar or related methods, as well as provide examples of current applications across the Agency. Drafts of both documents were released, with slightly different titles, for public comment and external peer review in August 2009. An external peer review was held in Arlington, Virginia in May 2010.

The goal of these publications is not only to describe potential and actual uses of these tools, but also to encourage their further implementation in human, ecological and environmental risk analysis and related decision making. The enhanced use of probabilistic analyses to characterize uncertainty in assessments will not only be responsive to external scientific advice (e.g., recommendations from the National Research Council) on how to further advance risk assessment science, but also will help to address specific challenges faced by managers and increase the confidence in the underlying analysis used to support Agency decisions.

Robert Kavlock
Interim Science Advisor
U.S. Environmental Protection Agency

Probabilistic Risk Analysis Technical Panel

Halûk Özkaynak, EPA Office of Research and Development (Co-Chair)
Robert Hetes, EPA Office of Research and Development (Co-Chair)
Kathryn Gallagher, EPA Office of Water (Co-Chair)
Chris Frey, North Carolina State University (while on temporary assignment at EPA) (White Paper Co-Lead)
John Paul, EPA Office of Research and Development (White Paper Co-Lead)
Pasky Pascual, EPA Office of Research and Development (White Paper Co-Lead)
Marian Olsen, EPA Region 2 (Case Study Lead)
Mike Clipper, EPA Office of Solid Waste and Emergency Response
Michael Messner, EPA Office of Water
Keeve Nachman, currently at The Johns Hopkins Bloomberg School of Public Health
Zachary Pekar, EPA Office of Air and Radiation
Rita Schoeny, EPA Office of Research and Development
Cynthia Stahl, EPA Region 3
David Hrdy, EPA Office of Pesticide Programs
John Langstaff, EPA Office of Air and Radiation
Elizabeth Margosches, EPA Office of Chemical Safety and Pollution Prevention (retired)
Audrey Galizia, EPA Office of Research and Development
Nancy Rios-Jafolla, EPA Region 3
Donna Randall, EPA Office of Chemical Safety and Pollution Prevention
Khoan Dinh, EPA Office of Chemical Safety and Pollution Prevention (retired)
Harvey Richmond, EPA Office of Air and Radiation (retired)

Other Contributing Authors

Jonathan Chen, EPA Office of Chemical Safety and Pollution Prevention
Lisa Conner, EPA Office of Air and Radiation
Janet Burke, EPA Office of Research and Development
Allison Hess, EPA Region 2
Kelly Sherman, EPA Office of Chemical Safety and Pollution Prevention
Woodrow Setzer, EPA Office of Research and Development
Valerie Zartarian, EPA Office of Research and Development

EPA Risk Assessment Forum Science Coordinators

Julie Fitzpatrick, EPA Office of the Science Advisor
Gary Bangs, EPA Office of the Science Advisor (retired)

External Peer Reviewers

Scott Ferson (Chair), Applied Biomathematics
Annette Guiseppi-Elie, DuPont Engineering
Dale Hattis, Clark University
Igor Linkov, U.S. Army Engineer Research and Development Center
John Toll, Windward Environmental LLC

Table of Contents

List of Figures and Tables

Figures

Appendix Figures

Tables

Appendix Table

List of Acronyms and Abbreviations

1-D MCA	One-Dimensional Monte Carlo Analysis
2-D MCA	Two-Dimensional Monte Carlo Analysis
APEX	Air Pollutants Exposure Model
BBN	Bayesian Belief Network
CAA	Clean Air Act
CASAC	Clean Air Scientific Advisory Committee
CCA	Chromated Copper Arsenate
CPSC	Consumer Product Safety Commission
CRA	Cumulative Risk Assessment
CSFII	Continuing Survey of Food Intake by Individuals
CWA	Clean Water Act
DEEM	Dietary Exposure Evaluation Model
DRA	Deterministic Risk Assessment
DRES	Dietary Risk Evaluation System
ERA	Ecological Risk Assessment
EMAP	Environmental Monitoring and Assessment Program
EPA	U.S. Environmental Protection Agency
FACA	Federal Advisory Committee Act
FAQ	Frequently Asked Questions
FDA	U.S. Food and Drug Administration
FFDCA	Federal Food, Drug, and Cosmetic Act
FIFRA	Federal Insecticide, Fungicide, and Rodenticide Act
FQPA	Food Quality Protection Act
GAO	Government Accountability Office
HHRA	Human Health Risk Assessment
HI	Hazard Index
IPCC	Intergovernmental Panel on Climate Change
IRIS	Integrated Risk Information System
LHS	Latin Hypercube Sampling
LOAEL	Lowest-Observed-Adverse-Effect Level
LT	Long-Term
LT2	Long-Term 2 Enhanced Surface Water Treatment Rule
MCA	Monte Carlo Analysis
MCS	Monte Carlo Simulation
MEE	Microexposure Event Analysis
MOEs	Margins of Exposure
NAAQS	National Ambient Air Quality Standards
NAS	National Academy of Sciences
NERL	National Exposure Research Laboratory
NOAEL	No-Observed-Adverse-Effect Level
NRC	National Research Council
OAQPS	Office of Air Quality Planning and Standards
OAR	Office of Air and Radiation
OCSPP	Office of Chemical Safety and Pollution Prevention
OERR	Office of Emergency and Remedial Response
OGWDW	Office of Groundwater and Drinking Water
OMB	Office of Management and Budget
OP	Organophosphorus Pesticide

OPP	Office of Pesticide Programs
ORD	Office of Research and Development
OSA	Office of the Science Advisor
OSTP	Office of Science and Technology Policy
OSWER	Office of Solid Waste and Emergency Response
OW	Office of Water
PAH	Polycyclic Aromatic Hydrocarbon
PCB	Polychlorinated Biphenyl
PCCRARM	Presidential/Congressional Commission on Risk Assessment and Risk Management
PDP	Pesticide Data Program
PM	Particulate Matter
PRA	Probabilistic Risk Assessment
RAF	Risk Assessment Forum
RfC	Reference Concentration (Inhalation)
RfD	Reference Dose (Oral)
RIA	Regulatory Impact Analysis
RME	Reasonable Maximum Exposure
SAB	Science Advisory Board
SAP	Scientific Advisory Panel
SHEDS	Stochastic Human Exposure and Dose Simulation Model
SHEDS-PM	Stochastic Human Exposure and Dose Simulation Model for Particulate Matter
STPC	Science and Technology Policy Council
TRIM.Expo	Total Risk Integrated Methodology/Exposure Model
UI	Uncertainty Interval
USDA	U.S. Department of Agriculture
USGS	U.S. Geological Survey
WHO	World Health Organization

EXECUTIVE SUMMARY

Probabilistic risk assessment (PRA), in its simplest form, is a group of techniques that incorporate uncertainty and variability into risk assessments. Variability refers to the inherent natural variation, diversity and heterogeneity across time, space or individuals within a population or lifestage, while uncertainty refers to imperfect knowledge or a lack of precise knowledge of the physical world, either for specific values of interest or in the description of the system (USEPA 2011c). Variability and uncertainty have the potential to result in overestimates or underestimates of the predicted risk.

PRA provides estimates of the range and likelihood of a hazard, exposure or risk, rather than a single point estimate. Stakeholders inside and outside of the Agency have recommended a more complete characterization of risks, including uncertainties and variability, in protecting more sensitive or vulnerable populations and lifestages. PRA can be used to support risk management by assessment of impacts of uncertainties on each of the potential decision alternatives.

Numerous advisory bodies, such as the Science Advisory Board (SAB) and the National Research Council (NRC) of the National Academy of Sciences (NAS), have recommended that EPA incorporate probabilistic analyses into the Agency's decision-making process. EPA's Risk Assessment Forum (RAF) formed a Technical Panel, consisting of representatives from the Agency's program and regional offices, to develop this white paper and its companion document, titled *Probabilistic Risk Assessment to Inform Decision Making: Frequently Asked Questions* (FAQ). The RAF is recommending the development of Agency resources, such as a clearinghouse of PRA case studies, best practices, resources and seminars, to raise general knowledge about how these probabilistic tools can be used.

The intended goal of this white paper is to explain how EPA can use probabilistic methods to address data, model and scenario uncertainty and variability by capitalizing on the wide array of tools and methods that comprise PRA. This white paper describes where PRA can facilitate more informed risk management decision making through better understanding of uncertainty and variability related to Agency decisions. The information contained in this document is intended for both risk analysts and managers faced with determining when and how to apply these tools to inform their decisions. This document does not prescribe a specific approach but, rather, describes the various stages and aspects of an assessment or decision process in which probabilistic assessment tools may add value.

Probabilistic Risk Assessment

PRA is an analytical methodology used to incorporate information regarding uncertainty and/or variability into analyses to provide insight regarding the degree of certainty of a risk estimate and how the risk estimate varies among different members of an exposed population, including sensitive populations or lifestages. Traditional approaches, such as deterministic analyses, often report risks as "central tendency," "high end" (e.g., 90th percentile or above) or "maximum anticipated exposure," but PRA can be used to describe more completely the uncertainty surrounding such estimates and identify the key contributors to variability or uncertainty in predicted exposures or risk estimates. This information then can be used by decision makers to achieve a science-based level of safety, to compare the risks related to different management options, or to invest in research with the greatest impact on risk estimate uncertainty.

To support regulatory decision making, PRA can provide information to decision makers on specific questions related to uncertainty and variability. For example, in the context of a decision analysis that has been conducted, PRA can: identify "tipping points" where the decision would be different if the risk estimates were different; estimate the degree of confidence in a particular decision; and help to estimate trade-offs related to different risks or management options. PRA can provide useful (even critical) information about the uncertainties and variability in the data, models, scenario, expert judgments and values incorporated in risk assessments to support decision making across the Agency.

PRA is applicable to both human health risk assessment (HHRA) and ecological risk assessment (ERA); however, there are differences between how PRA is used for the two. Both HHRA and ERA have a similar structure and use the same risk assessment steps, but HHRA focuses on individuals, a single species, morbidity and mortality, but ERA is more concerned with multiple populations of organisms (e.g., individual species of fish in a river) or ecological integrity (e.g., will the types of species living in the river change over time). In ERA, there also is a reliance on indicators of impacts (e.g., sentinel species and other metrics).

Risk Assessment at EPA

PRA began playing an increasingly important role in Agency risk assessments following the 1997 release of EPA's *Policy for Use of Probabilistic Analysis in Risk Assessment at the U.S. Environmental Protection Agency* (USEPA 1997a) and publication of the *Guiding Principles for Monte-Carlo Analysis* (USEPA 1997b). PRA was a major focus in an associated review of EPA risk assessment practices by the SAB (USEPA 2007b). The NRC recommended that EPA adopt a "tiered" approach for selecting the level of detail used in uncertainty and variability assessment (NRC 2009). Furthermore, the NRC recommended that a discussion about the level of detail used for uncertainty analysis and variability assessment should be an explicit part of the planning, scoping and problem formulation step in the risk assessment process. Both this white paper and the companion FAQ document take into account recommendations on risk assessment processes described in the NRC's report *Science and Decisions: Advancing Risk Assessment* (NRC 2009) and *Environmental Decisions in the Face of Uncertainty* (IOM 2013).

EPA's recent risk assessment publications, including the document titled *Framework for Human Health Risk Assessment to Inform Decision Making* (UAEPA 2014b) as well as this white paper, emphasize the importance of communicating the results of a PRA because it provides the range and likelihood estimates for one or more aspects of hazard, exposure or risk, rather than a single point estimate. Risk assessors are responsible for sharing information on probabilistic results so that decision makers have a clear understanding of quantitative assessments of uncertainty and variability, and how this information will affect the decision. Effective communication between the risk assessor and decision maker is key to promote understanding and use of the results from the PRA.

PRA generally requires more resources than standard Agency default-based deterministic approaches. Appropriately trained staff and the availability of adequate tools, methods and guidance are essential for the application of PRA. Proper application of probabilistic methods requires not only software and data, but also guidance and training for analysts using the tools, and for managers and decision makers tasked with interpreting and communicating the results. In most circumstances, probabilistic assessments may take more time and effort to conduct than conventional approaches, primarily because of the comprehensive inclusion of available information on model inputs. The potentially higher resource costs may be offset, however, by a more informed decision than would be provided by a comparable deterministic analysis.

Content of the White Paper and Frequently Asked Questions Companion Documents

These two documents describe how PRA can be applied to enhance the scientific foundation of EPA's decision making across the Agency. This white paper describes the challenges faced by EPA decision makers, defines and explains the basic principles of probabilistic analysis, briefly highlights instances where these techniques have been implemented in EPA decisions, and describes criteria that may be useful in determining whether and how the application of probabilistic methods may be useful and/or applicable to decision making. This white paper also describes commonly employed methods to address uncertainty and variability, including those used in the consideration of uncertainty in scenarios and uncertainty in models. Additionally, it addresses uncertainty and variability in the inputs and outputs of models and the impact of these uncertainties on each of the potential management options. A general description of the range of methods from simple to complex, rapid to more time consuming and least to most resource intensive is provided, as well as uses of these methods.

Both documents address issues such as uncertainty and variability, their relevance to decision making and the PRA goal to provide quantitative characterization of the uncertainty and variability in estimates of hazard, exposure, or risk. The difference between the white paper and the FAQs document is the level of detail provided about PRA concepts and practices, and the intended audience (e.g., risk assessors vs. decision makers). Detailed examples of applications of these methods are provided in the Appendix of this white paper, which is titled "Case Study Examples of the Application of Probabilistic Risk Analysis in U.S. Environmental Protection Agency Decision Making." The white paper Appendix includes 16 case studies—11 HHRA and 5 ERA examples—that illustrate how EPA's program and regional offices have used probabilistic techniques in risk assessment. To aid in describing how these tools were applied, the 16 case studies are subdivided among 3 categories for purposes of this document. Group 1 includes 2 case studies demonstrating point estimate, including sensitivity analysis; Group 2 is comprised of 5 case studies demonstrating probabilistic risk analysis, including one-dimensional Monte Carlo analysis and probabilistic sensitivity analysis; and Group 3 includes 9 case studies demonstrating advanced probabilistic risk analysis, including two-dimensional Monte Carlo analysis with micro exposure (micro environments) modeling, Bayesian statistics, geostatistics and expert elicitation.

The FAQ document provides answers to common questions regarding PRA, including key concepts such as scientific and institutional motivations for the use of PRA, and challenges in the application of probabilistic techniques. The principal reason for including PRA as an option in the risk assessor's toolbox is its ability to support the refinement and improvement of the information leading to decision making by incorporating known uncertainties.

3

1. INTRODUCTION: RELEVANCE OF UNCERTAINTY TO DECISION MAKING: HOW PROBABILISTIC APPROACHES CAN HELP

1.1. EPA Decision Making

To discuss where probabilistic approaches can aid EPA's decision making, it is important to generally describe the Agency's current decision-making processes and how better understanding and improving elements within these processes can clarify where probabilistic approaches might provide benefits. The enhanced use of PRA and characterization of uncertainty would allow EPA decision makers opportunities to use a more robust and transparent process, which may allow greater responsiveness to outside comments and recommendations. Such an approach would support higher quality EPA assessments and improve confidence in Agency decisions.

There are two major areas in the decision-making process that might be improved with PRA. Scientists currently are generally focused on the first area—the understanding of data, model and scenario uncertainties and variability. The second area is one that has not, until recently and only in a limited fashion, been used by EPA decision makers. This area is formal decision analysis. With decision analytic techniques, decision makers can weigh the relative importance of risk information compared to other information in making the decision, understand how uncertainty affects the relative attractiveness of potential decision alternatives, and assess overall confidence in a decision. In addition to data, model and scenario uncertainty, there is a separate category of uncertainties specifically associated with how the decision criteria relate to the decision alternatives. Although it is quite relevant to risk management decisions, the topic and decision analysis in general are outside of the scope of this report. This white paper focuses on technical information that would allow better understanding of the relationships among alternative decisions in assessing risks.

1.2. The Role of Probabilistic Risk Analysis in Characterizing Uncertainty and Variability

Probabilistic analyses include techniques that can be applied formally to address both uncertainty and variability, typically arising from limitations of data, models or adequately formulating the scenarios used in assessing risks. Probability is used in science, business, economics and other fields to examine existing data and estimate the chance of an event, from health effects to rain to mental fatigue. One can use probability (chance) to quantify the frequency of occurrence or the degree of belief in information. For variability, probability distributions are interpreted as representing the relative frequency of a given state of the system (e.g., that the data are distributed in a certain way); for uncertainty, they represent the degree of belief or confidence that a given state of the system exists (e.g., that we have the appropriate data; Cullen and Frey 1999). PRA often is defined narrowly to indicate a statistical or thought process used to analyze and evaluate the variability of available data or to look at uncertainty across data sets.

For the purposes of this document, PRA is a term used to describe a process that employs probability to incorporate variability in data sets and/or the uncertainty in information (such as data or models) into analyses that support environmental risk-based decision making. PRA is used here broadly to include both quantitative and qualitative methods for dealing with scenario, model and input uncertainty. Probabilistic techniques can be used with other types of analysis, such as benefit-cost analysis, regulatory impact analysis and engineering performance standards; thus, they can be used for a variety of applications and by experts in many disciplines.

4

1.3. Goals and Intended Audience

The primary goals of this white paper are to introduce PRA, describe how it can be used to better inform and improve the decision-making process, and provide case studies where it has been used in human health and ecological analyses at EPA (see the Appendix for the case studies). A secondary goal of this paper is to bridge communication gaps regarding PRA among analysts of various disciplines, between these analysts and Agency decision makers, and among affected stakeholders. This white paper also is intended to serve as a communication tool to introduce key concepts and background information on approaches to risk analysis that incorporate uncertainty and provide a more comprehensive treatment of variability. Risk analysts, decision makers and affected stakeholders can benefit from understanding the potential uses of PRA. PRA and related approaches can be used to identify additional research that may reduce uncertainty and more thoroughly characterize variability in a risk assessment. This white paper explains how PRA can enhance the decision-making processes faced by managers at EPA by better characterizing data, model, scenario and decision uncertainties.

1.4. Overview of This Document

This white paper provides an overview of EPA's interest and experience in addressing uncertainty and variability using probabilistic methods in risk assessment; identifies key questions asked or faced by Agency decision makers; demonstrates how conventional deterministic approaches to risk analysis may not answer these questions fully; provides examples of applications; and shows how and why "probabilistic risk analysis" (broadly defined) could provide added value, compared to traditional methods, with regard to regulatory decision making by more fully characterizing risk estimates and exploring decision uncertainties. For the purposes of this white paper, PRA and related tools for both human health and ecological assessments include a range of approaches, from statistical tools, such as sensitivity analysis, to multi-dimensional Monte Carlo models, geospatial approaches and expert elicitation. Key points addressed by this document include definitions and key concepts pertaining to PRA, benefits and challenges of PRA, a general conceptual framework for PRA, conclusions regarding products and insights obtained from PRA, and examples where EPA has used PRA in human health and ecological analyses. A Glossary and a Bibliography also are provided.

1.5. What Are Common Challenges Facing EPA Risk Decision Makers?

EPA operates under statutory and regulatory constraints that often limit the types of criteria that can be considered (including whether the use of PRA is appropriate) and impose strict timeframes in which decisions must be made. Typically, the decision begins with understanding (1) who or what will be protected; (2) the relationship between the data and decision alternatives; and (3) the impact of data, model and decision uncertainties related to each decision alternative. These are among the considerations of the planning and scoping and problem formulation phases of risk assessment (US EPA 2014). EPA decision makers need to consider multiple decision criteria, which are informed by varying degrees of confidence in the underlying information. Decision makers need to balance the regulatory/ statutory requirements and timeframes, resources (i.e., expertise, costs of the analysis, review times, etc.) to conduct the assessment, management options, and stakeholders while at the same time keeping risk assessment and decision making separate.

Uncertainty can be introduced into any assessment at any step in the process, even when using highly accurate data with the most sophisticated models. Uncertainty can be reduced or better characterized through knowledge. Variability or natural heterogeneity is inherent in natural systems and therefore cannot be reduced, but can be examined and described. Uncertainty in decisions is unavoidable because real-world situations cannot be perfectly measured, modeled or predicted. As a result, EPA decision makers face scientifically complex problems that are compounded by varying levels of uncertainty and variability. If uncertainty and variability have not been well characterized or acknowledged, potential complications arise in the process of decision making. Increased uncertainty can make it more difficult to determine, with reasonable confidence, the balance point between the costs of regulation and the implications for avoiding damages and producing benefits. Characterization facilitated by probabilistic analyses can provide insight into weighing the relative costs and benefits of varying levels of regulation and also can assist in risk communication activities.

Decision makers often want to know who is at risk and by how much, the tradeoffs between alternative actions and the likely or possible consequences of decisions. To this end, it is particularly useful for decision makers to understand the distribution of risk across potentially impacted populations and ecological systems. It can be important to know the number of individuals experiencing different magnitudes of risk, the differences in risk magnitude experienced by individuals in different lifestages or populations or the probability of an event that may lead to unacceptable levels of risk. Given the limitations of data, traditional methods of risk analyses are not well suited to produce such estimates. Probabilistic analytical methods are capable of addressing these shortcomings and can contribute to a more thorough recognition of the impact of data gaps on the projected risk estimates. Although PRA can be used to characterize the uncertainty and variability in situations with limited data, currently there is not extensive experience using PRA to characterize the range of effects or dose-response relationships for populations, including sensitive populations and lifestages.

Other challenges facing EPA decision makers include the need to consider multiple decision criteria, which are informed by varying degrees of confidence in the underlying information, understanding the relationship between and among those decision criteria (including multi-pollutant and multi-media effects) and the decision alternatives, and the timeliness of the decision making. Furthermore, even when PRA is used, EPA decision makers must be mindful of potential misuses and obfuscations when conducting or presenting PRA results. Decision makers also need to consider the evolving science behind PRA. As the use of PRA increases decision makers will become more familiar with the techniques and their application.

A risk assessment process needs to consider uncertainties, variability and the rationale or factors influencing how they may be addressed by a decision maker. Decision makers need a foundation for estimating the value of collecting additional information to allow for better informed decisions. There are costs associated with ignoring uncertainty (McConnell 1997 and Toll 1999), and a focus by decision makers on the information provided by uncertainty analysis can strengthen their choices.

1.6. What Are Key Uncertainty and Variability Questions Often Asked by Decision Makers?

As described above, determining the decision-making context and specific concerns is a critical first step toward developing a useful and responsive risk assessment that will support the decision. For example, the appropriate focus and level of detail of the analysis should be commensurate with the needs of the decision maker and stakeholders, as well as the appropriate use of science. Analyses often are conducted at a level of detail dictated by the issue being addressed, the breadth and quality of the available information upon which to base an analysis, and the significance surrounding a decision. The analytical process tends to be iterative. Although a guiding set of questions may frame the initial analyses, additional questions can arise that further direct or even reframe the analyses.

Based on a series of discussions with Agency decision makers and risk assessors, some typical questions about uncertainty and variability relevant to risk analyses including:

❐ Factors influencing decision uncertainty:

- Would my decision be different if the data were different, improved or expanded? Would additional data collection and research likely lead to a different decision? How long will it take to collect the information, how much would it cost, and would the resulting decision be significantly altered?
- What are the liabilities and consequences of making a decision under the current level of knowledge and uncertainty?
- How do the alternatives and their associated uncertainty and variability affect the target population or lifestage?

❐ Considerations for evaluating data or method uncertainty:

- How representative or conservative is the estimate due to data or method uncertainty (also incorporating variability)?
- What are the major gaps in knowledge, and what are the major assumptions used in the assessment? How reasonable are the assumptions?

❐ Issues arising when addressing variability:

- Can a probabilistic approach (e.g., to better characterize uncertainties and variability) be accomplished in a timely manner?
- What is the desired percentile of the population to be protected? By choosing this percentile, who may not be protected?

The questions that arise concerning uncertainty and variability change depending on the stage and nature of the decision-making process and analysis. General phases of the risk assessment process are illustrated in Figure 1. For further information on the process of decision making, we suggest referring to the description provided by EPA Region 3 on the Multi-Criteria Integrated Resource

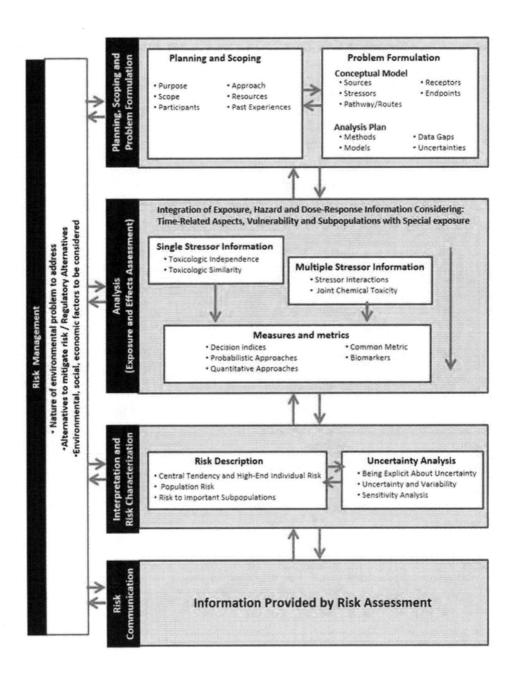

Figure 1. General Phases of the Risk Assessment Process. Risk assessment is an iterative process comprised of planning, scoping and problem formulation; analysis (e.g., hazard identification, dose-response assessment and exposure assessment); interpretation and risk characterization; and risk communication. The highlighted boxes explain how PRA fits into the overall process.

Assessment Internet page at http://www.epa.gov/reg3esd1/data/mira.htm. The utility of various levels of analysis and sophistication in answering these questions is illustrated in the case studies described in Section 1.10 and presented in the Appendix of this white paper. References to examples beyond these EPA case studies can be found in the Bibliography. Additionally, Lester *et al.* (2007) identified more than 20 PRA application case studies (including EPA examples) performed since 2000; these case study examples are categorized as site-specific applications and regional risk assessments.

1.7. Why Is the Implementation of Probabilistic Risk Analysis Important?

The principal reason for the inclusion of PRA as an option in the risk assessor's toolbox is PRA's ability to support refinement and improvement of the information leading to decision making by incorporating known uncertainties. Beginning as early as the 1980s, expert scientific advisory groups, such as the National Research Council (NRC), recommended that risk analyses include a clear discussion of the uncertainties in risk estimation (NRC 1983). The NRC stated the need to describe uncertainty and to capture variability in risk estimates (NRC 1994). The Presidential/ Congressional Commission on Risk Assessment and Risk Management (PCCRARM) recommended against a requirement or need for a "bright line" or single-number level of risk (PCCRARM 1997). See Section 2.4 for more information regarding the scientific community's opinion on the use of PRA.

Regulatory science often requires selection of a limit for a contaminant, yet that limit always contains uncertainty as to how protective it is. PRA and related tools quantitatively describe the very real variations in natural systems and living organisms, how they respond to stressors, and the uncertainty in estimating those responses.

Risk characterization became EPA policy in 1995 (USEPA 1995b), and the principles of transparency, clarity, consistency and reasonableness are explicated in the 2000 *Risk Characterization Handbook* (USEPA 2000a). Transparency, clarity, consistency and reasonableness criteria require decision makers to describe and explain the uncertainties, variability and known data gaps in the risk analysis and how they affect the resulting decision-making processes (USEPA 1992, 1995a, 2000a).

The use of probabilistic methods also has received support from some decision makers within the Agency, and these methods have been incorporated into a number of EPA decisions to date. Program offices, such as the Office of Pesticide Programs (OPP), Office of Solid Waste and Emergency Response (OSWER), Office of Air and Radiation (OAR), and Office of Water (OW), as well as the Office of Research and Development (ORD), have utilized probabilistic approaches in different ways and to varying extents, for both human exposure and ecological risk analyses. In addition, OSWER has provided explicit guidance on the use of probabilistic approaches for exposure analysis (USEPA 2001). Some program offices have held training sessions on Monte Carlo simulation (MCS) software that is used frequently in probabilistic analyses.

The NRC recommended that EPA should adopt a tiered approach for selecting the level of detail used in uncertainty and variability assessment (NRC 2009). Furthermore, NRC recommended that a discussion about the level of detail used for uncertainty analysis and variability assessment should be an explicit part of the planning, scoping and problem formulation step in the risk assessment process. The way that PRA fits into a graduated hierarchical (tiered) approach is more fully described in Section 2.10 and illustrated in Figure 2.

When it is beneficial to refine risk estimates, the use of PRA can help in the characterization and communication of uncertainty, variability and the impact of data gaps in risk analyses for assessors, decision makers and stakeholders (including the target population or lifestage).

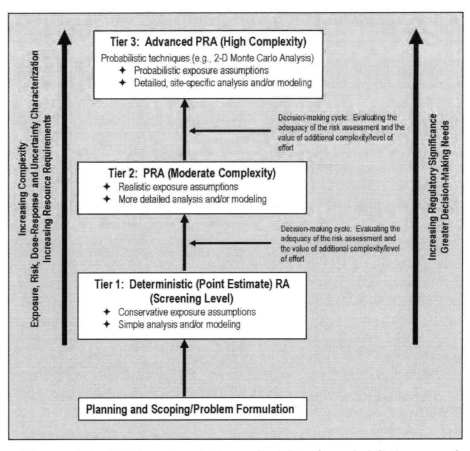

Figure 2. Tiered Approach for Risk Assessment. The applicability of a probabilistic approach depends on the needs of decision makers and stakeholders. Assessments that are high in complexity and regulatory significance benefit from the application of probabilistic techniques.
Source: Adapted from USEPA 2004a and WHO 2008.

1.8. How Does EPA Typically Address Scientific Uncertainty and Variability?

Environmental assessments can be complex, such as covering exposure to multiple chemicals in multiple media for a wide-ranging population. The Agency has developed simplified approaches to characterize risks associated with such complex assessments through the use of point estimates for model variables or parameters. Such an approach typically produces point estimates of risks (e.g., 10^{-5} or a lifetime probability of cancer risk of one individual in 100,000). These often are called "deterministic" assessments. As a result of the use of point estimates for variables in model algorithms, deterministic risk results usually are reported as what are assumed to be either average or worst-case estimates. They do not contain any quantitative estimate of the uncertainty in that estimate, nor report what percentile of the exposed population the estimate applies. The methods typically used in EPA risk assessments rely on a combination of point values with potentially varying levels of conservatism and certainty, yielding a point estimate of exposure at some point in the range of possible risks.

Because uncertainty is inherent in all risk assessments, it is important that the risk assessment process enable handling uncertainties in a logical way that is transparent and scientifically defensible, consistent with the Agency's statutory mission and responsive to the needs of decision makers (NRC 1994). Uncertainty is a factor in both ecological and human health risk assessments.

For human health risk assessments, uncertainties arise for both noncancer and cancer endpoints. Thus, when data are missing, EPA often uses several options to provide boundaries on uncertainty and variability in an attempt to avoid risk underestimation; attempting to give a single quantification of how much confidence there is in the risk estimate may not be informative or feasible.

In exposure assessment, for example, the practice at EPA is to collect new data where they are needed and where time and resources allow. Alternative approaches to address uncertainty include narrowing the scope of the assessment; using screening-level default assumptions that include upper-end values and/or central tendency values that are generally combined to generate risk estimates that fall within the higher end of the population risk range (USEPA 2004b); applying models to estimate missing values; using surrogate data (e.g., data on a parameter that come from a different region of the country than the region being assessed); or applying professional judgment. The use of individual assumptions can range from qualitative (e.g., assuming that one is secured to the residence location and does not move through time or space) to more quantitative (e.g., using the 95th percentile of a sample distribution for an ingestion rate). This approach also can be applied to the practice of hazard identification and dose-response assessment when data are missing. Identifying the sensitivity of exposure or risk estimates to key inputs can help focus efforts to reduce uncertainty by collecting additional data.

Current EPA practices to address uncertainty and variability are focused on the evaluation of data, model, and scenario uncertainty and variability. In addition, decision makers are faced with combining many different decision criteria that may be informed by science and PRA as well as by expert judgment or the weighting of values to choose a decision alternative. Data, model, and scenario uncertainties and variability (including their probability distributions), as well as expert judgment, can be important considerations in the selection of one alternative over another (Costanza *et al.* 1997; Morgan *et al.* 2009; Stahl and Cimorelli 2005; Wright *et al.* 2002).

1.9. What Are the Limitations of Relying on Default-Based Deterministic Approaches?

Default-based deterministic approaches are applied to data, model and scenario uncertainties. Deterministic risk assessment (DRA) often is considered a traditional approach to risk analysis because of the existence of established guidance and procedures regarding its use, the ease with which it can be performed, and its limited data and resource needs. The use of defaults supporting DRA provides a procedural consistency that allows for risk assessments to be feasible and tractable. Decision makers and members of the public tend to be relatively familiar with DRA, and the use of such an approach addresses assessment-related uncertainties primarily through the incorporation of predetermined default values and conservative assumptions. It addresses variability by combining input parameters intended to be representative of typical or higher end exposure (i.e., considered to be conservative assumptions). The intention often is to implicitly provide a margin of safety (i.e., more likely to overestimate risk than underestimate risk) or construct a screening-level estimate of high-end exposure and risk (i.e., an estimate representative of more highly exposed and susceptible individuals).

DRA provides an estimation of the exposures and resulting risks that addresses uncertainties and variabilities in a qualitative manner. The methods typically used in EPA DRA rely on a combination of point values—some conservative and some typical—yielding a point estimate of exposure that is at some unknown point in the range of possible risks. Although this conservative bias aligns with the public health mission of EPA (USEPA 2004b), the degree of conservatism in these risk estimates (and in any concomitant decision) cannot be estimated well or communicated (Hattis and Burmaster 1994). Typically, this results in unquantified uncertainty in risk statements.

Quantitative information regarding the precision or potential systematic error and the distribution of exposures, effects and resulting risks across different members of an exposed population are usually not provided with estimates generated using default approaches. Although DRA may present qualitative information regarding the robustness of the estimates, the impact of data and model limitations on the quality of the results cannot be quantified. Reliance on deterministically derived estimations of risk can result in decision making based solely on point estimates with an unknown degree of conservatism, which can complicate the comparison of risks or management options.

In risk assessments of noncancer endpoints, metrics such as an oral reference dose (RfD) and an inhalation reference concentration (RfC) are typically used. The use of conservative defaults long has been the target of criticism (Finkel 1989) and has led to the presumption by critics that EPA assessments are overly conservative and unrealistic. The use of PRA would be advantageous in eliminating a single value and might be less likely to imply undue precision and lessen the need for conservative assumptions, thereby reducing bias in the estimate. In the probabilistic framework, a probability distribution would be used to express the belief that any particular value represents the dose or exposure concentration that would pose no appreciable risk of adverse effects (NRC 2009). EPA is investigating the use of PRA to derive risk values for RfD and RfC in EPA's Integrated Risk Information System (IRIS) Database (www.epa.gov/IRIS/).

EPA commissioned a white paper (Hattis and Lynch 2010) presented at the Hazardous Air Pollutant Workshop, 2009, illustrating the implementation of probabilistic methods in defining RfDs and assessing the benefits for reducing exposure to toxicants that act in part through traditional individual threshold processes. The use of PRA, among other things, makes provision for interactions with background pathological processes, as recommended by the NRC (2009), and shows how the system can inform assessments for "data-poor" toxicants.

PRA may be more suitable than DRA for complex assessments, including those of aggregate and cumulative exposures and time-dependent individual exposure, dose and effects analyses. Identification and prioritization of contributory sources of uncertainty can be difficult and time consuming when using deterministic methods, leading to difficulties in model evaluation and the subsequent appraisal of risk estimates (Cullen and Frey 1999). Quantitative analyses of model sensitivities are essential for the prioritization of key uncertainties—a critical process in identifying steps for data collection or research to improve exposure or risk estimates.

1.10. What Is EPA's Experience with the Use of Probabilistic Risk Analysis?

EPA's experience with PRA has, to date, primarily been limited to the evaluation of data, model and scenario uncertainties. To assist with the growing number of probabilistic analyses of exposure data in these uncertainty areas, EPA issued *Guiding Principles for Monte Carlo Analysis* (USEPA 1997b). Given adequate supporting data and credible assumptions, probabilistic analysis techniques, such as Monte Carlo analysis, can be viable statistical tools for analyzing uncertainty and variability in risk assessments. EPA's policy for the use of probabilistic analysis in risk assessment, released in 1997, is inclusive of human exposure and ecological risk assessments and does not rule out probabilistic health effects analyses (USEPA 1997a). Subsequently, EPA's SAB and Scientific Advisory Panel (SAP) have reviewed PRA approaches to risks used by EPA offices such as OAR, OPP and others. Several programs have developed specific guidance on the use of PRA, including OPP and OSWER (USEPA 1998a, 2001).

To illustrate the practical application of PRA to problems relevant to the Agency, several example case studies are briefly described here. The Appendix titled Case Study Examples of *Application of*

Probabilistic Risk Analysis in U.S. Environmental Protection Agency Regulatory Decision Making, discusses these and other case studies in greater detail, including the procedures and outcomes. The Appendix includes 16 case studies—11 HHRA and 5 ERA examples—that are intended to illustrate how some of EPA's programs and offices currently utilize PRA. To aid in describing how probabilistic analyses were used, the 16 case studies are subdivided among 3 categories of PRA tools: Group 1—point estimate, including sensitivity analysis; Group 2—probabilistic risk analysis, including one-dimensional Monte Carlo analysis (1-D MCA) and probabilistic sensitivity analysis; and Group 3—advanced probabilistic risk analysis, including two-dimensional Monte Carlo analysis (2-D MCA) with microexposure (microenvironments) modeling, Bayesian statistics, geostatistics and expert elicitation .

It is useful to note that the NRC (2009) recommended a tiered approach to risk assessment using both qualitative and quantitative (deterministic and probabilistic) tools, with the complexity of the analysis increasing as progress is made through the tiers. The use of PRA tools to address issues of uncertainty and variability in a tiered approach is described more completely in Section 2.10 and was illustrated in Figure 2. The three tiers illustrated in that figure approximately correspond to the three groups of EPA case studies described in the Appendix that provide examples of the use of various PRA tools.

Table A-1 in the Appendix offers a summary of the 16 case studies based on the type of risk assessment, the PRA tools used in the assessment, and the EPA program or regional office responsible for the assessment. Some of the approaches that are profiled in these case studies can be used in the planning and scoping phases of risk assessments and risk management. Other, more complex PRA approaches are used to answer more specific questions and provide a richer description of the risks. Most studies show that PRA can improve or expand on information generated by deterministic methods. In some of the case studies, the use of multiple PRA tools is illustrated. For example, Case Study 1 describes the use of a point estimate sensitivity analysis to identify exposure variables critical to the analysis summarized in Case Study 9. Both of these case studies focus on children's exposure to chromated copper arsenate (CCA)-treated wood. In Case Study 9, an MCA was used as an example of a two-dimensional (i.e., addressing both variability and uncertainty) probabilistic exposure assessment.

Overall, the case studies illustrate that the Agency already has applied the science of PRA to ecological risk and human exposure estimation and has begun using PRA to describe health effects. Some of the applications have used existing "off-the-shelf" software, whereas others have required significant effort and resources. Once developed, however, some of the more complex models have been used many times for different assessments. All of the assessments have been validated by internal and external peer review. Table 1 gives some highlights the case studies from deterministic to more complex assessments, which are described in more detail in the Appendix.

Table 1. Selected Examples of EPA Applications of Probabilistic Risk Assessment Techniques

Case Study No.	Description	Group	Type of Risk Assessment	Office/Region
2	**Atmospheric Deposition to Watershed Contamination:** The Office of Research and Development (ORD) developed an analysis of nitrogen, mercury and polycyclic aromatic hydrocarbons (PAHs) depositions toward watershed contamination in the Casco Bay Estuary in southwestern Maine.	Group 1: Point Estimate	Ecological	ORD
5	**Hudson River Polychlorinated Biphenyl (PCB)-Contaminated Sediment Site:** Region 2 evaluated the variability in risks to anglers who consume recreationally caught fish contaminated with PCBs from sediment contamination in the Hudson River.	Group 2: 1-D Monte Carlo Analysis	Human Health	Superfund/ Region 2 (New York)
7	**Environmental Monitoring and Assessment Program (EMAP):** ORD developed and the Office of Water (OW) applied probabilistic sampling techniques to evaluate the Nation's aquatic resources under the Clean Water Act (CWA) Section 305(b).	Group 2: Probabilistic Sensitivity Analysis	Ecological	ORD/OW
9	**Chromated Copper Arsenate (CCA) Risk Assessment:** ORD and the Office of Pesticide Programs (OPP) conducted a probabilistic assessment of children's exposure (addressing both variability and uncertainty) to arsenic and chromium from contact with CCA-treated wood play sets and decks.	Group 3: 2-D Monte Carlo Analysis	Human Health	ORD/OPP
13	**Evaluating Ecological Effects of Pesticide Uses:** OPP developed a probabilistic model, which evaluates acute mortality levels in generic and specific ecological species for user-defined pesticide uses and exposures.	Group 3: Probabilistic Analysis	Ecological	OPP
14	**Fine Particulate Matter Health Impacts:** ORD and the Office of Air and Radiation (OAR) used expert elicitation to more completely characterize, both qualitatively and quantitatively, the uncertainties associated with the relationship between reduction in fine particulate matter ($PM_{2.5}$) and benefits of reduced $PM_{2.5}$-related mortality.	Group 3: Expert Elicitation	Human Health	ORD/OAR

2. PROBABILISTIC RISK ANALYSIS

2.1. What Are Uncertainty and Variability, and How Are They Relevant to Decision Making?

The concepts of uncertainty and variability are introduced here, and the relevance of these concepts to decision making is discussed.

2.1.1. Variability

Variability refers to real differences over time, space or members of a population and is a property of the system being studied (e.g., drinking water consumption rates for each of the many individual adult residents living in a specific location or differences in body lengths or weights for humans or ecological species) (Cullen and Frey 1999; USEPA 2011c). Variability can arise from inherently random processes, such as variations in wind speed over time at a given location or from true variation across members of a population that, in principle, could be explained, but which, in practice, may not be explainable using currently available models or data (e.g., the range of lead levels in the blood of children 6 years old or younger following a specific degree of lead exposure). Of particular interest in both HHRA and ERA is inter-individual variability, which typically refers to differences between members of the same population in either behavior related to exposure (e.g., dietary consumption rates for specific food items), or biokinetics related to chemical uptake (e.g., gastrointestinal uptake rates for lead following intake) or toxic response (e.g., differences among individuals or species in the internal dose needed to produce a specific amount of neurological impairment).

Inter-individual variability is illustrated in Case Study 5 in the Appendix, which assesses a PCB-contaminated sediment site in the Hudson River. In this case study, the quantification of variability is illustrated through the use of a PRA tool—1-D MCA—to describe the variability of exposure as a function of individual exposure factors (i.e., young children's fish ingestion).

2.1.2. Uncertainty

Uncertainty is the lack of knowledge of the true value of a quantity or relationships among quantities (USEPA 2011c). For example, there may be a lack of information regarding the true distribution of variability between individuals for consumption of certain food items. There are a number of types of uncertainties for both risk analysis. The following descriptions of the types of uncertainty (adapted from Cullen and Frey 1999) addresses uncertainties that arise during risk analyses. These uncertainties can be separated broadly into three categories: (1) scenario uncertainty; (2) model uncertainty; and (3) input or parameter uncertainty. Each of these is explained in the paragraphs that follow.

Scenario uncertainty refers to errors, typically of omission, resulting from incorrect or incomplete specification of the risk scenario to be evaluated. The risk scenario refers to a set of assumptions regarding the situation to be evaluated, such as: (1) the specific sources of chemical emissions or exposure to be evaluated (e.g., one industrial facility or a cluster of varied facilities impacting the same study area); (2) the specific receptor populations and associated exposure pathways to be modeled (e.g., indoor inhalation exposure, track-in dust or consumption of home-produced dietary items); and (3) activities by different lifestages to be considered (e.g., exposure only at home, or consideration of workplace or commuting exposure). Mis-specification of the risk scenario can result in underestimation, overestimation or other mischaracterization of risks. Underestimation may occur because of the exclusion of relevant situations or the inclusion of irrelevant situations with respect to a particular analysis. Overestimation may occur because of the inclusion of unrealistic or irrelevant situations (e.g., assuming continuous exposure to an intermittent airborne contaminant source rather than accounting for mobility throughout the day).

Model uncertainty refers to limitations in the mathematical models or techniques that are developed to represent the system of interest and often stems from: (1) simplifying assumptions; (2) exclusion of relevant processes; (3) mis-specification of model boundary conditions (e.g., the range of input parameters); or (4) misapplication of a model developed for other purposes. Model uncertainty typically arises when the risk model relies on missing or improperly formulated processes, structures or equations. Sources of model uncertainty are defined in the Glossary.

Input or parameter uncertainty typically refers to errors in characterizing the empirical values used as inputs to the model (e.g., engineering, physical, chemical, biological or behavioral variables). Input uncertainty can originate from random or systematic errors involved in measuring a specific phenomenon (e.g., biomarker measurements, such as the concentration of mercury in human hair); statistical sampling errors associated with small sample sizes (e.g., if the data are based on samples selected with a random, representative sampling design); the use of surrogate data instead of directly measured data; the absence of an empirical basis for characterizing an input (e.g., the absence of measurements for fugitive emissions from an industrial facility); or the use of summary measures of central tendency rather than individual observations. Nonlinear random processes can exhibit a behavior that, for small changes in input values, produces a large variation in results.

Input or parameter uncertainty is illustrated in Case Study 3 in the Appendix titled "Probabilistic Assessment of Angling Duration Used in the Assessment of Exposure to Hudson River Sediments via Consumption of Contaminated Fish." In this case study, a probabilistic analysis of one parameter in an exposure assessment—the time an individual spends fishing in a large river system—was assessed using sensitivity analysis. This analysis was conducted because there was uncertainty that the individual exposure duration based on residence duration may underestimate the time spent fishing (i.e., angling duration). The full distribution of the calculated values was used in conducting the 1-D MCA for the fish consumption pathway, which is presented in Case Study 5.

Decision uncertainty refers to a decision analysis that would include not only the impact of scenario, model and input uncertainties on the relative attractiveness of potential decision alternatives, but also would include the degree to which specific choices (such as selecting input data, models, and scenarios, and even how the problem or decision analysis is framed) impact the relative attractiveness of potential decision alternatives. In decision making, analysts use data to represent decision criteria that decision makers and other stakeholders believe will help them to answer their decision question(s). These questions might include which policy alternative best meets Agency goals (that must be articulated) or which risk assessment scenario best describes the observed effects. Data, model and scenario uncertainties will influence the risk assessment results and those, in turn, will influence the risk management options. Decision makers who understand the uncertainty associated with their specific choices can be more confident that the decision will produce the results that they seek. In addition, these decision makers will be able to defend their decisions better and explain how the decision meets Agency and stakeholder goals.

While this is beyond the scope of this document, Stahl and Cimorelli (2005 and 2012) illustrate how uncertainty throughout the decision making process can be assessed. These case studies explored the assessment of ozone monitoring networks and air quality management policies that seek to minimize the adverse impacts from ozone, fine particulate matter and air toxics simultaneously. These case studies demonstrate the importance and feasibility of better understanding the uncertainty introduced by specific choices (e.g., selecting input data, models, and scenarios) when making public policy decisions.

2.2. When Is Probabilistic Risk Analysis Applicable or Useful?

PRA may be particularly useful, for example, in the following (Cooke 1991; Cullen and Frey 1999; NRC 2009; USEPA 2001):

- ❑ When a screening-level DRA indicates that risks are possibly higher than a level of concern and a more refined assessment is needed.

- ❑ When the consequences of using point estimates of risk are unacceptably high.

- ❑ When significant equity or environmental justice issues are raised by inter-individual variability.

- ❑ To estimate the value of collecting additional information to reduce uncertainty.

- ❑ To identify promising critical control points and levels when evaluating management options.

- ❑ To rank exposure pathways, sites, contaminants and so on for the purposes of prioritizing model development or further research.

- ❑ When combining expert judgments on the significance of the data.

- ❑ When exploring the impact of the probability distributions of stakeholder and decision-maker values on the attractiveness of potential decision alternatives (Fischhoff 1995; Illing 1999; Kunreuther and Slovic 1996; USEPA 2000b).

- ❑ When exploring the impact of the probability distributions of the data, model and scenario uncertainties, and variability together to compare potential decision alternatives.

PRA may add minimal value to the assessment in the following types of situations (Cullen and Frey 1999; USEPA 1997a):

- ❑ When a screening-level deterministic risk assessment indicates that risks are negligible, presuming that the assessment is known to be conservative enough to produce overestimates of risk.

- ❑ When the cost of averting the exposure and risk is smaller than the cost of a probabilistic analysis.

- ❑ When there is little uncertainty or variability in the analysis (this is a rare situation).

2.3. How Can Probabilistic Risk Analysis Be Incorporated Into Assessments?

As illustrated in the accompanying case studies in the Appendix, probabilistic approaches can be incorporated into any stage of a risk assessment, from problem formulation or planning and scoping to the analysis of alternative decisions. In some situations, PRA can be used selectively for certain components of an assessment. It is common in assessments that some model inputs are known with high confidence (i.e., based on site-specific measurements), whereas values for other inputs are less certain (i.e., based on surrogate data collected for a different purpose). For example, an exposure modeler may determine that relevant air quality monitoring data exists, but there is a lack of detailed information on human activity patterns in different microenvironments. Thus, an assessment of the variability in exposure to airborne pollutants might be based on direct use of the monitoring data, whereas assessment of uncertainty and variability in the inhalation exposure component might be based on statistical analysis of surrogate data or use of expert judgment. The uncertainties are likely to be larger for the latter than the former component of the assessment;

17

efforts to characterize uncertainties associated with pollutant exposures would focus on the latter. PRA also deals with dependency issues; a description of these issues is available in Section 3.3.2.

2.4. What Are the Scientific Community's Views on Probabilistic Risk Analysis, and What Is the Institutional Support for Its Use in Performing Assessments?

The NRC and IOM recently emphasized their long-standing advocacy for PRA (NRC 2007a and b; IOM 2013). Dating from its 1983 *Risk Assessment in the Federal Government: Managing the Process* (NRC 1983)—which first formalized the risk assessment paradigm—through reports released from the late 1980s through the early 2000s, various NRC panels have maintained consistently that because risk analysis involves substantial uncertainties, these uncertainties should be evaluated within a risk assessment. These panels noted that:

1. When evaluating the total population risk, EPA should consider the distribution of exposure and sensitivity of response in the population (NRC 1989).

2. When assessing human exposure to air pollutants, EPA should present model results along with estimated uncertainties (NRC 1991).

3. When conducting ERA, EPA should discuss thoroughly uncertainty and variability within the assessment (NRC 1993).

4. "Uncertainty analysis is the only way to combat the 'false sense of certainty,' which is *caused* by a refusal to acknowledge and [attempt to] quantify the uncertainty in risk predictions," as stated in the NRC report, *Science and Judgment in Risk Assessment* (NRC 1994).

5. EPA's estimation of health benefits was not wholly credible because EPA failed to deal formally with uncertainties in its analyses (NRC 2002).

6. EPA should adopt a "tiered" approach for selecting the level of detail used in uncertainty and variability assessment. Furthermore, the NRC recommended that a discussion of the level of detail used for uncertainty analysis and variability assessment should be an explicit part of the planning, scoping and problem formulation phase of the risk assessment process (NRC 2009).

7. EPA should develop methods to systematically describe and account for uncertainties in decision-relevant factors in addition to estimates of health risk in its decision-making process (IOM 2013).

Asked to recommend improvements to the Agency's HHRA practices, EPA's SAB echoed the NRC's sentiments and urged the Agency to characterize uncertainty and variability more fully and systematically and to replace single-point uncertainty factors with a set of distributions using probabilistic methods (Parkin and Morgan 2007). The key principles of risk assessment cited by the Office of Science and Technology Policy (OSTP) and the Office of Management and Budget (OMB) include "explicit" characterization of the uncertainties in risk judgments; they proceed to cite the National Academy of Science's (NAS) 2007 recommendation to address the "variability of effects across potentially affected populations" (OSTP/OMB 2007).

18

2.5. Additional Advantages of Using Probabilistic Risk Analysis and How It Can Provide More Comprehensive, Rigorous Scientific Information in Support of Regulatory Decisions.

External stakeholders previously have used the Administrative Procedure Act and the Data Quality Act to challenge the Agency for a lack of transparency and consistency or for not fully analyzing and characterizing the uncertainties in risk assessments or decisions (Fisher *et al.* 2006). The more complete implementation of PRA and related approaches to deal with uncertainties in decision making would address stakeholder concerns in regard to characterizing uncertainties.

The results of any assessment, including PRA, are dependent on the underlying methods and assumptions. Accompanied by the appropriate documentation, PRA may communicate a more robust representation of risks and corresponding uncertainties. This characterization may be in the form of a range of possible estimates as opposed to the more traditionally presented single-point values. Depending on the use of the assessment, ranges can be derived for variability and uncertainty (or a combination of the two) in both model inputs and resulting estimations of risk.

PRA quantifies how exposures, effects and risks differ among human populations or lifestages or target ecological organisms. PRA also provides an estimation of the degree of confidence with which these estimates may be made, given the current uncertainty in scientific knowledge and available data. A 2007 NRC panel stated that the objective of PRAs is *not* to decide "how much evidence is sufficient" to adopt an alternative but, rather, to describe the scientific bases of proposed alternatives so that scientific and policy considerations may be more fully evaluated (NRC 2007a). EPA's SAB similarly noted that PRAs provide more "value of information" through a quantitative assessment of uncertainty and clarify the science underlying Agency decisions (USEPA 2007b).

The SAB articulated a number of advantages for EPA decision makers from the utilization of probabilistic methods (Parkin and Morgan 2007):

❏ A probabilistic reference dose could help reduce the potentially inaccurate implication of zero risk below the RfD.

❏ By understanding and explicitly accounting for uncertainties underlying a decision, EPA can estimate formally the value of gathering more information. By doing so, the Agency can better prioritize its information needs by investing in areas that yield the greatest information value.

❏ Strategic use of PRA would allow EPA to send the appropriate signal to the intellectual marketplace, thereby encouraging analysts to gather data and develop methodologies necessary for assessing uncertainties.

2.6. What Are the Challenges to Implementation of Probabilistic Analyses?

Currently, EPA is using PRA in a variety of programs to support decisions, but challenges remain regarding the expanded use of these tools within the Agency. The challenges include:

❏ A lack of understanding of the value of PRA for decision making. PRA helps to improve the rigor of the decision-making process by allowing decision makers to explore the impacts of uncertainty and variability on the decision choices.

❏ A clear institutional understanding of how to incorporate the results of probabilistic analyses into decision making is lacking.

❏ PRA typically requires a different skill set than used in current evaluations, and limited resources (staff, time, training or methods) to conduct PRA are available.

❏ Communicating probabilistic analysis results and the impact of those results on the decision/policy options can be complex.

❏ Communication with stakeholders is often difficult and results in the appearance of regulatory delays due the necessity of analyzing numerous scenarios using various models.

❏ PRA complicates decision making and risk communication in instances where a more comprehensive characterization of the uncertainties leads to a decrease in clarity regarding how to estimate risk for the scenario under consideration. These challenges are discussed in more detail in Sections 2.7 through 2.13.

2.7. How Can Probabilistic Risk Analysis Support Specific Regulatory Decision Making?

Decision makers sometimes perceive that the binary nature of regulatory decisions (e.g., Does an exposure exceed a reference dose or not? Do emissions comply with Agency standards or not?) precludes the use of a risk range developed through PRA. Generally, it is necessary to explain the rationale underlying a particular decision. PRA's primary purpose is to provide information to enhance the ability to make transparent decisions based on the best available science. By conducting a sensitivity analysis of the influence of the uncertainty on the decision-making process, it can be determined how or if PRA can help to improve the process.

PRA can provide information to decision makers on specific questions related to uncertainty and variability. For questions of uncertainty and to minimize the likelihood of unintended consequences, PRA can help to provide the following types of information:

❏ Characterization of the uncertainty in estimates (i.e., What is the degree of confidence in the estimate?). Could the prediction be off by a factor of 2, a factor of 10 or a factor of 1,000?

❏ Critical parameters and assumptions that most affect or influence a decision and the risk assessment.

❏ "Tipping points" where the decision would be altered if the risk estimates were different, or if a different assumption was valid.

❏ Estimate the likelihood that values for critical parameters will occur or test the validity of assumptions.

❏ Estimate the degree of confidence in a particular decision and/or the likelihood of specific decision errors.

❏ The possibility of alternative outcomes with additional information, or estimate tradeoffs related to different risks or risk-management decisions.

❏ The impact of additional information on decision making, considering the cost and time to obtain the information and the resulting change in decision (i.e., the value of the information).

For the consideration of variability, PRA can help to provide the following types of information for exposures:

❏ Explicitly defined exposures for various populations or lifestages (i.e., Who are we trying to protect?). That is, will the regulatory action keep 50 percent, 90 percent, 99.9 percent or some other fraction of the population below a specified exposure, dose or risk target?

□ Variability in the exposures, among various populations or lifestages, and information on the percentile of the population that is being evaluated in the risk assessment (e.g., variations in the number of liters of water per kilogram [kg] body weight per day consumed by the population). This information is helpful in addressing comments:

- On the conservatism of EPA's risk assessments;

- Concerns about whether their particular exposures were evaluated in the risk assessment;

- Whom or what is being protected by implementing a decision; and

- Whether and what additional research may be needed to reduce uncertainty.

PRA helps to inform decisions by characterizing the alternatives available to the decision maker and the uncertainty he or she faces, and by providing evaluation measures of outcomes. Uncertainties often are represented as probabilities or probability distributions numerically or in graphs. As part of a decision analysis, stakeholders can more fully examine how uncertainties influence the preference among alternatives.

2.8. Does Probabilistic Risk Analysis Require More Resources Than Default-Based Deterministic Approaches?

PRA generally can be expected to require more resources than standard Agency default-based deterministic approaches. There is extensive experience within EPA in conducting and reviewing DRA. These assessments tend to follow standardized methods that minimize the effort required to conduct them and to communicate the results. Probabilistic assessments often entail a more detailed analysis, and as a result, these assessments require substantially more resources, including time and effort, than do deterministic approaches.

Appropriately trained staff and the availability of adequate tools, methods and guidance are essential for the application of PRA. Proper application of probabilistic methods requires not only software and data, but also guidance and training for analysts using the tools and for managers and decision makers tasked with interpreting and communicating the results.

An upfront increase in resources needed to conduct a probabilistic assessment can be expected, but development of standardized approaches and/or methods can lead to the routine incorporation of PRA in Agency approaches (e.g., OPP's use of the Dietary Exposure Evaluation Model [DEEM; http://www.epa.gov/pesticides/science/deem/], a probabilistic dietary exposure model). The initial and, in some cases, ongoing resource cost (e.g., for development of site-specific models for site assessments) may be offset by a more informed decision than a comparable deterministic analysis. Probabilistic methods are useful for identifying effective management options and prioritizing additional data collection or research aimed at improving risk estimation, ultimately resulting in decisions that enable improved environmental protection while simultaneously conserving more resources.

2.9. Does Probabilistic Risk Analysis Require More Data Than Conventional Approaches?

There are differences of opinion within the technical community as to whether PRA requires more data than other types of analyses. Although some emphatically believe that PRA requires more data, others argue that probabilistic assessments make better use of all of the available data and information. Stahl and Cimorelli (2005) discuss when and how much data are necessary for a decision. PRA can benefit from more data than might be used in a DRA. For example, where DRA might employ selected point estimates (e.g., the mean or 95th percentile values) from available data sets for use in model inputs, PRA facilitates the use of frequency-weighted data distributions, allowing for a more comprehensive consideration of the available data. In many cases, the data that were used to develop the presumptive 95th percentile can be employed in the development of probabilistic distributions.

Restriction of PRA to principally data-rich situations may prevent its broader application where it is most useful. Because PRA incorporates information on data quality, variability and uncertainty into risk models, the influence of these factors on the characterization of risk can become a greater focus of discussion and debate.

A key benefit of using PRA is its ability to reveal the limitations as well as the strengths of data that often are masked by a deterministic approach. In doing so, PRA can help to inform research agendas, as well as support regulatory decision making, based on the state of the best available science. In summary, PRA typically requires more time for developing input assumptions than a DRA, but when incorporated into the relevant steps of the risk assessment process, PRA can demonstrate added benefits. In some cases, PRA can provide additional interpretations that compensate for the extra effort required to conduct a PRA.

2.10. Can Probabilistic Risk Analysis Be Used to Screen Risks or Only in Complex or Refined Assessments?

Probabilistic methods typically are not necessary where traditional default-based deterministic methods are adequate for screening risks. Such methods are relatively low cost, intended to produce conservatively biased estimates, and useful for identifying situations in which risks are so low that no further action is needed. The application of probabilistic methods can be targeted to situations in which a screening approach indicates that a risk may be of concern or when the cost of managing the risk is high, creating a need for information to help inform decision making. PRA fits directly into a graduated hierarchical approach to risk analysis. This tiered approach, depicted in Figure 2, is a process for a systematic informed progression to increasingly more complex risk assessment methods, depending on the decision-making context and need. Higher tiers reflect increasing complexity and often will require more time and resources. An analysis might typically start at a lower tier and only progress to a higher tier if there is a need for a more sophisticated assessment commensurate with the importance of the problem. Higher tiers also reflect increasing characterization of variability and/or uncertainty in the risk estimate, which may be important for risk-management decisions. The case studies described in the Appendix are presented in three groups that generally correspond to the tiers identified in Figure 2. Group 1 case studies are point estimate (sensitivity analysis) examples (Tier 1); Group 2 case studies include most moderate-complexity PRA examples (Tier 2); and Group 3 case studies are advanced (high complexity) PRA examples (Tier 3).

The tiered approach in Figure 2 depicts a continuum from screening level point estimate that is done with little data and conservative assumptions to PRA that requires an extensive data set and more realistic (less conservative) assumptions. In between, there can be a wide variety of tiers of increasing complexity, or there may be only a few reasonable choices between screening methods and highly refined analyses (USEPA 2004a). A similar four-tiered approach for characterizing the variability and/or uncertainty in the estimated exposure or risk analysis (WHO 2008) has been adapted by EPA in the risk and exposure assessments conducted for the National Ambient Air Quality Standards (NAAQS).

PRA also could be used to examine more fully the existing default-based methods based on the current state of information and knowledge to determine if such methods are truly conservative and adequate for screening (e.g., in dose-response analyses dealing with hazard characterization) (Swartout *et al.* 1998; Hattis *et al.* 2002).

The use of a spectrum of data should be employed both in determining screening risks and in more complex assessments. For HHRA, data from human, animal, mechanistic and other studies should be used to develop a probabilistic characterization of cancer and noncancer risks and to identify uncertainties. The NRC recommended that EPA facilitate this approach by redefining RfD and RfC within the probabilistic framework to take into account the probability of harm (NRC 2009). It is likely that both DRA and PRA will be part of this framework.

2.11. Does Probabilistic Risk Analysis Present Unique Challenges to Model Evaluation?

The concept of "validation" of models used for regulatory decision making has been a topic of intense discussion. In a recent report on the use of models in environmental regulatory decision making, the NRC recommended using the notion of model "evaluation" rather than "validation," suggesting that use of a process that encompasses the entire life cycle of the model and incorporates the spectrum of interested parties in the application of the model often extends beyond the model builder and decision maker. Such a process can be designed to ensure that judgment of the model application is based not only on its predictive value determined from comparison with historical data, but also on its comprehensiveness, rigor in development, transparency and interpretability (NRC 2007b).

Model evaluation is important in all risk assessments. In the case of PRA, there is an additional question as to the validity of the assumptions regarding probability and frequency distributions for model inputs and their dependencies. Probabilistic information can be accounted for during evaluation analyses by considering the range of uncertainty in the model prediction and whether such a range overlaps with the "true" value based on independent data. Thus, probabilistic information can aid in characterizing the precision of the model predictions and whether a prediction is significantly different from a benchmark of interest. For example, comparisons of probabilistic model results and monitoring data were performed for multiple models in developing the cumulative pesticide exposure model. Concurrent PRA model evaluations using a Bayesian analysis also have been published (Clyde 2000).

When risk assessors develop models of risk, they rely on two predominant statistical methods. Both methods arise from axioms of probability, but each applies these axioms differently. Under the frequentist approach, one develops and evaluates a model by testing whether the model—as applied to the observations—conforms to idealized distributions. Under the Bayesian approach, one develops and evaluates a model by testing which—among alternative models—best yields the underlying distribution describing the data. The practical differences between these two approaches can perhaps best be appreciated when considering the structural uncertainty in models (Section 3.3.3). Because Bayesians estimate model parameters with the expectation that these parameters—or even model structures—will be updated as new data become available, they have developed formal techniques to provide uncertainty bounds around these parameter estimates, select models that best explain the given data, or combine the results of alternative models.

2.12. How Do You Communicate the Results of Probabilistic Risk Analysis?

Effective communication makes it easier for regulators and stakeholders to understand the decision criteria driving the decision-making process. In other words, communication of PRA results within the decision-making context facilitates understanding. The specific approaches for reporting results from PRA vary depending on the assessment objective and the intended audience. Beyond the basic 1997 principles and the policy from the same year (USEPA 1997a and b), the *Risk Assessment Guidance for Superfund: Volume III—Part A, Process for Conducting Probabilistic Risk Assessment* also provides some guidance on the quality and criteria for acceptance as well as communication basics (USEPA 2001). There have been limited studies of how information from PRA regarding uncertainty and variability can or should be communicated to key audiences, such as decision makers and stakeholders (e.g., Morgan and Henrion 1990; Bloom *et al.* 1993; Krupnick *et al.* 2006). Among the analyst community, there often is an interest in visualization of the structure of a scenario and model using influence diagrams and depiction of the uncertainty and variability in model inputs and outputs using probability distributions in the form of cumulative density functions or probability distribution functions (Figure 3). Sensitivity of the model output to uncertainty and variability in model inputs can be depicted using graphical tools.

In some cases, these graphical methods can be useful for those less familiar with PRA, but in many cases there is a need to translate the quantitative results into a message that extracts the key insights without burdening the decision maker with obscure technical details. In this regard, the use of ranges of values for a particular metric of decision-making relevance (e.g., the range of uncertainty associated with a particular estimate of risk) may be adequate. The presentation of PRA results to a decision maker may be conducted best as an interactive discussion, in which a principal message is conveyed, followed by exploration of issues such as the source, quality and degree of confidence associated with the information. There is a need for the development of recommendations and a communication plan regarding how to communicate the results of PRA to decision makers and stakeholders, building on the experience of various programs and regions.

2.13. Are the Results of Probabilistic Risk Analysis Difficult to Communicate to Decision Makers and Stakeholders?

Research has shown that the ability of decision makers to deal with concepts of probability and uncertainty varies. Bloom *et al.* (1993) surveyed a group of senior managers at EPA and found that many could interpret information about uncertainty if it was communicated in a manner responsive to decision-maker interests, capabilities and needs. In a more recent survey of ex-EPA officials, Krupnick *et al.* (2006) concluded that most had difficulty understanding information on uncertainty with conventional scientific presentation approaches. The findings of these studies highlight the need for practical strategies for the communication of results of PRA and uncertainty information between risk analysts and decision makers, as well as between decision makers and other stakeholders. The Office of Emergency and Remedial Response (OERR) has compiled guidance to assist analysts and managers in understanding and communicating the results of PRA (USEPA 2001).

Risk analysts need to focus on how to use uncertainty analysis to characterize how confident decision makers should be in their choices. As Wilson (2000) explained, "... uncertainty is the bane of any decision maker's existence. Thus, anyone who wants to inform decisions using scientific information needs to assure that their analyses transform uncertainty into confidence in conclusions." Hence, although environmental risk assessments are complicated and it is easy to get lost in the details, presenting and discussing these results within the context of the decision facilitates understanding. The translation of uncertainty into confidence statements forces a "top-down" perspective that promotes accounting for whether and how uncertainties affect choices (Toll *et al.* 1997).

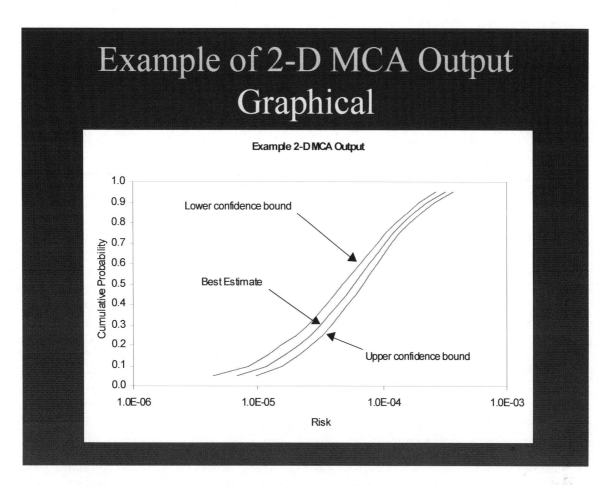

Figure 3. Graphical Description of the Likelihood (Probability) of Risk. Hypothetical fitted data distribution with upper and lower confidence intervals are depicted for the output of a 2-D MCA model.

3. AN OVERVIEW OF SOME OF THE TECHNIQUES USED IN PROBABILISTIC RISK ANALYSIS

3.1. What Is the General Conceptual Approach in Probabilistic Risk Analysis?

PRA includes several major steps, which parallel the accepted environmental health risk assessment process. These include: (1) problem and/or decision criteria identification; (2) gathering information; (3) interpreting the information; (4) selecting and applying models and methods for quantifying variability and/or uncertainty; (5) quantifying inter-individual or population uncertainty and variability in metrics relevant to decision making; (6) sensitivity analysis to identify key sources of variability and uncertainty; and (7) interpreting and reporting results.

Problem formulation entails identifying the assessment endpoints or issues that are relevant to the decision-making process and stakeholders, and that can be addressed in a scientific assessment process. Following problem formulation, information is needed from stakeholders and experts regarding the scenarios to evaluate. Based on the scenarios and assessment endpoints, the analysts select or develop models, which in turn leads to identification of model input data requirements and acquisition of data or other information (e.g., expert judgment encoded as the result of a formal elicitation process) that can be used to quantify inputs to the models. The data or other information for model inputs is interpreted in the process of developing probability distributions to represent variability, uncertainty or both for a particular input. Thus, steps (1) through (4) listed above are highly interactive and iterative in that the data input requirements and how information is to be interpreted depend on the model formulation, which depends on the scenario and that in turn depends on the assessment objective. The assessment objective may have to be refined depending on the availability of information.

Once a scenario, model and inputs are specified, the model output is estimated. A common approach is to use Monte Carlo Analysis (MCA) or other probabilistic methods to generate samples from the probability distributions of each model input, run the model based on one random value from each probabilistic input, and produce one corresponding estimate of the model outputs. This process is repeated typically hundreds or thousands of times to create a synthetic statistical sample of model outputs. These output data are interpreted as a probability distribution of the output of interest. Sensitivity analysis can be performed to determine which model input distributions are most highly associated with the range of variation in the model outputs. The results may be reported in a wide variety of forms depending on the intended audience, ranging from qualitative summaries to tables, graphs and diagrams.

Detailed introductions to PRA methodology are available elsewhere, such as Ang and Tang (1984), Cullen and Frey (1999), EPA (2001), and Morgan and Henrion (1990). A few key aspects of PRA methodology are briefly mentioned here. Readers who seek more detail should consult these references and see the Bibliography for additional references.

3.2. What Levels and Types of Probabilistic Risk Analyses Are There and How Are They Used?

There are multiple levels and types of analysis used to conduct risk assessments (illustrated in Figure 2 and Table 1, respectively). Graduated approaches to analysis are widely recognized (e.g., USEPA 1997a, 2001; WHO 2008). The idea of a graduated approach is to choose a level of detail and refinement for an analysis that is appropriate to the assessment objective, data quality, information available and importance of the decision (e.g., resource implications).

As discussed in section 1.8, there is a variety of approaches to risk assessment that differ in their complexity and the manner in which they address uncertainty and variability. In DRA one does not formally characterize uncertainty or variability but rather typically relies on using default-based assumptions and factors to generate a single estimate of risk. In PRA there is a variety of approaches to explicitly address or characterize uncertainty or variability in risk estimates and these differ in terms of how they accomplish this, the data used, and the overall complexity. Some examples are:

- Sensitivity analysis
- Monte Carlo analysis of variability in exposure data
- Human health or ecological effects data
- Monte Carlo analysis of uncertainty
- "Cumulative" PRA—multi-pathway or multi-chemical
- Two-dimensional PRA of uncertainty and variability
- Decision uncertainty analysis
- Geospatial analysis
- Expert elicitation

The DRA approaches described in Section 1.8 are examples of lower levels in a graduated approach to analysis. Risk at the lower levels of analysis is assessed by conservative, bounding assumptions. If the risk estimate is found to be very low despite the use of conservative assumptions, then there exists a great deal of certainty that the actual risks to the population of interest for the given scenario are below the level of concern and no further intervention is required, assuming that the scenario and model specifications are correct. When a conservative DRA indicates that a risk may be high, it is possible that the risk estimate is biased and the actual risk may be lower. In such a situation, depending on the resource implications of the decision, it may be appropriate to proceed with a more refined or higher level of analysis. The relative costs of intervention versus further analysis should be considered when deciding whether to proceed with a decision based on a lower level analysis or to escalate to a higher level of analysis. In some deterministic assessments (e.g., ecological risks), the assumptions are not well assured of conservatism, and the estimated risks might be biased to appear lower than the unseen actual risk.

A more refined analysis could involve the application of DRA methods, but with alternative sets of assumptions intended to characterize central tendency and reasonable upper bounds of exposure, effects and risk estimates, such that the estimates could be for an actual individual in the population of interest rather than a hypothetical maximally exposed individual. Such analyses are not likely to provide quantification regarding the proportion of the population at or below a particular exposure or risk level of concern, uncertainties for any given percentile of the exposed population, or priorities among input assumptions with respect to their contributions to uncertainty and variability in the estimates.

To more fully answer the questions often asked by decision makers, the analysis can be further refined by incorporating quantitative comparisons of alternative modeling strategies (to represent structural uncertainties associated with scenarios or models), quantifying ranges of uncertainty and variability in model outputs, and providing the corresponding ranges for model outputs of interest. When performing probabilistic analyses, choices are made regarding whether to focus on the quantification of variability only, uncertainty only, both variability and uncertainty together (representing a randomly selected individual), or variability and uncertainty independently (e.g., in a two-dimensional depiction of probability bands for estimates of inter-individual variability; see Figure 4). The simultaneous but distinct propagation of uncertainty and variability in a two-dimensional framework enables quantification of uncertainty in the risk for any percentile of the population. For example, one could estimate the range of uncertainty in the risk faced by the median member of the population or the 95th percentile member of the population. Such information can be used by a decision maker to gauge the confidence that should be placed in any particular estimate of risk, as well as to determine whether additional data collection or information might be useful to reduce the uncertainty in the estimates. The OPP assessment of Chromated Copper Arsenate-treated wood used such an approach. (See Case Study 9 in the Appendix.)

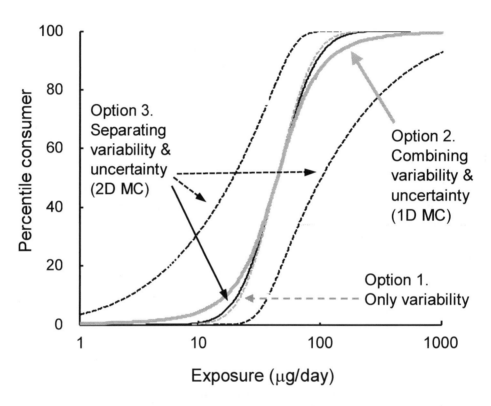

Figure 4. Diagrammatic Comparison of Three Alternative Probabilistic Approaches for the Same Exposure Assessment. In Option 1 (one dimensional Monte Carlo analysis), only variability is quantified. In Option 2 (one dimensional Monte Carlo analysis), both uncertainty and variability are combined. In Option 3 (two dimensional Monte Carlo analysis), variability and uncertainty are analyzed separately. Source: WHO 2008.

When conducting an analysis for the first time, it may not be known or clear, prior to analysis, which components of the model or which model inputs contribute the most to the estimated risk or its uncertainty and variability. As a result of completing an analysis, however, the analyst often gains insight into the strengths and weaknesses of the models and input information. Probabilistic analysis and sensitivity analysis can be used together to identify the key sources of quantified uncertainty in the model outputs to inform decisions regarding priorities for additional data collection. Ideally, time should be allowed for collecting such information and refining the analysis to arrive at a more representative and robust estimate of uncertainty and variability in risk. Thus, the notion of *iteration* in developing and improving an analysis is widely recommended.

The notion of iteration can be applied broadly to the risk assessment framework. For example, a first effort to perform an analysis may lead to insight that the assessment questions might be impossible to address, or that there are additional assessment questions that may be equally or more important. Thus, iteration can include reconsideration of the initial assessment questions and the corresponding implications for definition of scenarios, selection of models and priorities for obtaining data for model inputs. Alternatively, in a time-limited decision environment, probabilistic and sensitivity analyses may offer insight into the effect of management options on risk estimates.

3.3. What Are Some Specific Aspects of and Issues Related to Methodology for Probabilistic Risk Analysis?

This section briefly describes a few key aspects of PRA, model development and associated uncertainties. Detailed introductions to PRA methodology are available elsewhere, such as Ang and Tang (1984), Morgan and Henrion (1990), Cullen and Frey (1999) and EPA (2001). For more detailed information, consult these references and see the Bibliography for additional sources.

3.3.1. Developing a Probabilistic Risk Analysis Model

There are two key issues that should be considered in developing a PRA model; as discussed below.

Structural Uncertainty in Scenarios

A potentially key source of uncertainty in an analysis is the scenario, which includes specification of pollutant sources, transport pathways, exposure routes, timing and locations, geographic extent and related issues. There is no formalized methodology for dealing quantitatively with uncertainty and variability in scenarios. Decisions regarding what to include or exclude from a scenario could be recast as hypotheses regarding which agents, pathways, microenvironments, etc., contribute significantly to the overall exposure and risk of interest. In practice, however, the use of qualitative methods to frame an assessment tends to be more common, given the absence of a formal quantitative methodology.

Coupled Models

For source-to-outcome risk assessments, it often is necessary to work with multiple models, each of which represents a different component of a scenario. For example, there may be separate models for emissions, air quality, exposure, dose and effects. Such models may have different spatial and temporal scales. When conducting an integrated assessment, there may be significant challenges and barriers to coupling such models into one coherent framework. Sometimes, the coupling is done dynamically in a software environment. In other cases, the output of one model might be processed manually to prepare the information for input to the next model. Furthermore, there may be feedback between components of the scenario (e.g., poor air quality might affect human activity, which, in turn, could affect both emissions and exposures) that are incompletely captured or not included. Thus, the coupling of multiple models can be a potentially significant source of structural uncertainty (Özkaynak 2009).

3.3.2. Dealing With Dependencies Among Probabilistic Inputs

When representing two or more inputs to a model as probability distributions, the question arises as to whether it is reasonable to assume that the distributions are statistically independent. If there is a dependence, it could be as simple as a linear correlation between two inputs, or it could be more complicated, such as nonlinear or nonmonotonic relationships. Dependencies typically are not important if the risk estimate or other model output is sensitive to one or none of the probabilistic inputs that might have interdependence. Furthermore, dependencies typically are not of practical importance if they are weak. When dependencies exist and might significantly influence the risk estimate, they can be taken into account using a variety of statistical simulation methods or, perhaps more appropriately, by modeling the dependence analytically where possible. Details on methods for assessing the importance of possible dependencies and of quantifying them when needed are described in Ferson *et al.* (2004 and 2009).

For some types of models, such as air quality models, it is not possible to introduce a probability distribution to one input (e.g., ambient temperature at a particular location) without affecting variables at other locations or times (e.g., temperatures in other locations at the same times or temporal trends in temperature). In such cases, it is better to produce an "ensemble" of alternative temperature fields, each of which is internally consistent. Individual members of an ensemble usually are not interpreted as representing a probability sample; however, comparison of multiple ensembles of meteorological conditions, for example, can provide insight into natural sources of variability in ambient concentrations.

3.3.3. Conducting the Probabilistic Analysis

<u>Quantifying Uncertainty and Variability in Model Inputs and Parameters</u>

After the models are selected or developed to simulate a scenario of interest, attention typically turns to the development of input data for the model. There is a substantial amount of literature regarding the application of statistical methods for quantifying uncertainty and variability in model inputs and parameters based on empirical data (e.g., Ang and Tang 1984; Cullen and Frey 1999; Morgan and Henrion 1990; USEPA 2001). For example, a commonly used method for quantifying variability in a model input is to obtain a sample of data, select a type of parametric probability distribution model to fit to the data (e.g., normal, lognormal or other form), estimate the parameters of the distribution based on the data, critique the goodness-of-fit using graphical (e.g., probability plot) and statistical (e.g., Anderson-Darling, Chi-Square or Kolmogorov-Smirnov tests) methods and choose a preferred fitted distribution. This methodology can be adjusted to accommodate various types of data, such as data that are samples from mixtures of distributions or that contain non-detected (censored) values. Uncertainties can be estimated based on confidence intervals for statistics of interest, such as mean values, or the parameters of frequency distributions for variability. Various texts and guidance documents, both Agency and programmatic, describe these approaches, including the *Guiding Principles for Monte Carlo Analysis* (USEPA 1997b).

The most common method for estimating a probability distribution in the output of a model, based on probability distributions specified for model inputs, is MCS (Cullen and Frey 1999; Morgan and Henrion 1990). MCS is popular because it is very flexible. MCS can be used with a wide variety of probability distributions as well as different types of models. The main challenge for MCS is that it requires repetitive model calculations to construct a set of pseudo-random numbers for model inputs and the corresponding estimates for model outputs of interest. There are alternatives to MCS that are similar but more computationally efficient, such as Latin Hypercube Sampling (LHS). Techniques are available for simulating correlations between inputs in both MCS and LHS. For models with very simple functional forms, it may be possible to use exact or approximate analytical calculations, but such situations are encountered infrequently in practice. There may be situations in which the data do not conform to a well-defined probability distribution. In such cases, algorithms (such as Markov Chain Monte Carlo) can estimate a probability distribution by calculating a mathematical form describing the pattern of observed data. This form, called the likelihood function, is a key component of Bayesian inference and, therefore, serves as the basis for some of the analytical approaches to uncertainty and variability described below.

The use of empirical data presumes that the data comprise a representative, random sample. If known biases or other data quality problems exist, or if there is a scarcity or absence of relevant data, then naïve reliance on available empirical data is likely to result in misleading inferences in the analysis. Alternatively, estimates of uncertainty and variability can be encoded, using formal protocols, based on elicitation of expert judgment (e.g., Morgan and Henrion 1990, USEPA 2011a). Elicitation of expert judgment for subjective probability distributions is used in situations where there are insufficient data to support a statistical analysis of uncertainty, but in which there is sufficient knowledge on the part of experts to make an inference regarding uncertainty. For example, EPA conducted an expert elicitation study on the concentration-response relationship between the annual average ambient less than 2.5 micrometer (μm) diameter particulate matter ($PM_{2.5}$) exposure and annual mortality (IEC 2006; see also Case Studies 6 and 14 in the Appendix). Subjective probability distributions that are based on expert judgment can be "updated" with new data as they become available using Bayesian statistical methods.

Structural Uncertainty in Models

There may be situations in which it proves useful to evaluate not just the uncertainties in inputs and parameter values, but also uncertainties regarding whether a model adequately captures—in a hypothesized, mathematical, structured form—the relationship under investigation. A qualitative approach to evaluating the structural uncertainty in a model includes describing the critical assumptions within a model, the documentation of a model or the model quality, and how the model fits the purpose of the assessment. Quantitative approaches to evaluating structural uncertainty in models are manifold. These include parameterization of a general model that can be reduced to alternative functional forms (e.g., Morgan and Henrion 1990), enumeration of alternative models in a probability tree (e.g., Evans *et al.* 1994), comparing alternative models by evaluating likelihood functions (e.g., Royall 1997; Burnham and Anderson 2002), pooling results of model alternatives using Bayesian model averaging (e.g., Hoeting *et al.* 1999) or testing the causal relationships within alternative models using Bayesian Networks (Pearl 2009).

Sensitivity Analysis: Identifying the Most Important Model Inputs

Probabilistic methods typically focus on how uncertainty or variability in a model input affect [or result in] with respect to uncertainty or variability in a model output. After a probabilistic analysis is completed, sensitivity analysis typically takes the perspective of looking back to evaluate how much of the variation in the model output is attributable to individual model inputs (e.g., Frey and Patil 2002; Mokhtari *et al.* 2006; Saltelli *et al.* 2004).

There are many types of sensitivity analysis methods, including simple techniques that involve changing the value of one input at a time and assessing the effect on an output, and statistical methods that evaluate which of many simultaneously varying inputs contribute the most to the variance of the model output. Sensitivity analysis can answer the following key questions:

- ❏ What is the impact of changes in input values on model output?
- ❏ How can variation in output values be apportioned among model inputs?
- ❏ What are the ranges of inputs associated with best or worst outcomes?
- ❏ What are the key controllable sources of variability?
- ❏ What are the critical limits (e.g., the emission reduction target)?
- ❏ What are the key contributors to the output uncertainty?

Thus, sensitivity analysis can be used to inform decision making.

Iteration

There are two major types of iteration in risk assessment modeling. One is iterative refinement of the type of analysis, perhaps starting with a relatively simple DRA as a screening step in an initial level of analysis and proceeding to more refined types of assessments as needed in subsequent levels of analysis. Examples of more refined levels of assessment include application of sensitivity analysis to DRA; the use of probabilistic methods to quantify variability only, uncertainty only, or combined variability and uncertainty (to represent a randomly selected individual); or the use of two-dimensional probabilistic methods for distinguishing and simultaneously characterizing both uncertainty and variability.

The other type of iteration occurs within a particular level and includes iterative efforts to formulate a model, obtain data and evaluate the model to prioritize data needs. For example, a model may require a large number of input assumptions. To prioritize efforts of specifying distributions for uncertainty and variability for model inputs, it is useful to determine which model inputs are the most influential with respect to the assessment endpoint. Therefore, sensitivity can be used based on preliminary assessments of ranges or distributions for each model input to determine which inputs are the most important to the assessment. Refined efforts to characterize distributions then can be prioritized to the most important inputs.

4. SUMMARY AND RECOMMENDATIONS

4.1. Probabilistic Risk Analysis and Related Analyses Can Improve the Decision-Making Process at EPA

PRA can provide useful (even critical) information about the uncertainties and variability in the data, models, scenario, expert judgments and values incorporated in risk assessments to support decision making across the Agency. As discussed in this paper PRA is an analytical methodology capable of incorporating information regarding uncertainty and/or variability in risk analyses to provide insight on the degree of certainty of a risk estimate and how the risk estimate varies within the exposed population. Traditional approaches such as DRA, often report risks using descriptors such as "central tendency," "high end" (e.g., 90th percentile or above) or "maximum anticipated exposure". By contrast PRA can be used to describe more completely the uncertainty surrounding such estimates, as well as to identify the key contributors to uncertainty and variability in predicted exposures or risk estimates. This information then can be used by decision makers to weigh alternatives, or to make decisions on whether to collect additional data, or to conduct additional research in order to reduce the uncertainty and further characterize variability within the exposed population. Information on uncertainties and variability in exposure and response can ultimately improve the risk estimates.

PRA can be used to obtain insight on whether one management alternative is more likely to reduce risks compared to another. In addition, PRA can facilitate the development of modeling scenarios and the simultaneous consideration of multiple model alternatives. Probabilistic methods offer a number of tools designed to increase confidence in decision making through the incorporation of input uncertainty and variability characterization and prioritization in risk analyses. For example, one PRA tool, sensitivity analyses can be used to identify influential knowledge gaps in the estimation of risk; this improves transparency in the presentation of these uncertainties and improves the ability to communicate the most relevant information more clearly to decision makers and stakeholders. PRA allows one to investigate potential changes in decisions that could result from the collection of additional information. However, the additional resources (e.g., time, costs, or expertise) to undertake need to be weighed against the potential improvements in the decision making process. Ultimately, PRA may enhance the scientific foundation of the EPA's approach to decision making.

The various tools and methods discussed in this white paper can be utilized at all stages of risk analysis and also can aid the decision-making process by, for example, characterizing inter-individual variability and uncertainties.

PRA and related methods are employed in varying degrees across the Agency. Basic guidance exists at EPA on the use and acceptability of PRA for risk estimation, but implementation varies greatly within programs, offices and regions .The use of Monte Carlo or other probability-based techniques to derive a range of possible outputs from uncertain inputs is a fairly well-developed approach within EPA. Although highly sophisticated human exposure assessment and ecological risk applications have been developed, the use of PRA models to assess human health effects and dose-response relationships has been more limited at the Agency.

The evaluation of the application of PRA techniques under specific laws and regulations varies by program, office and region. Moving forward, it is important to broaden discussions between risk assessors and risk managers regarding how PRA tools can be used to support specific decisions and how they can be used within the regulatory framework used by programs, offices, and regions to make decisions. This can be accomplished by expanding the dialogue between assessors and manages at all levels regarding how the PRA tools have been used and how they have enhanced decision making.

Increased use of PRA and consistent application of PRA tools in support of EPA decision making requires enhanced internal capacity for conducting these assessments, as well as improved interpretation and communication of such information in the context of decisions. Improvements of Agency capacity could be accomplished through sharing of experiences, knowledge and training and increased availability of tools and methods.

4.2. Major Challenges to Using Probabilistic Risk Analysis to Support Decisions

The challenges for EPA are two-fold. As an Agency responsible for protecting human health and the environment, EPA makes regulatory and policy decisions, even in the presence of conflicting stakeholder positions and the inevitable uncertainties in the science. The first challenge for EPA is to determine how to conduct its decision-making responsibilities, weighing determinations of what constitutes too much uncertainty to make a decision, against potential adverse consequences of postponing decisions.

The second challenge, is that although current PRA techniques are available that would help to inform EPA decision-making processes, research and guidance are needed to improve these methods for a more complete implementation of PRA in HHRA and ERA. In particular, additional guidance is needed to help analysts and decision makers better understand how to incorporate PRA approaches into the decision-making process. This includes, guidance on which statistical tools to use and when to use them, and how probabilistic information can help to inform the scientific basis of decisions. Both DRA and PRA as well as appropriate statistical methods may be useful at any stage of the risk analysis and decision-making process, from planning and scoping to characterizing and communicating uncertainty.

❑ As noted in Section 3.3, there are significant challenges in properly accounting for uncertainty and variability when multiple models are coupled together to represent the source-to-outcome continuum. Moreover, the coupling of multiple models might need to involve inputs and corresponding uncertainties that are incorporated into more than one model, potentially resulting in complex dependencies. Integrative research on coupled model uncertainties will be quite valuable.

❑ There may be mismatches in the temporal and spatial resolution of each model that confound the ability to propagate uncertainty and variability from one model to another. For some models, the key uncertainties may be associated with inputs, whereas for other models, the key uncertainties may be associated with structure or parameterization alternatives. Model integration and harmonization activities will be important to addressing these technical issues.

4.3. Recommendations for Enhanced Utilization of Probabilistic Risk Analysis at EPA

Some examples of areas where new or updated guidance would be helpful are these:

❑ Identification of different types of information required for the various Agency decision-making processes, such as data analysis, tools, models, and use of experts.

❑ Use of probabilistic approaches to evaluate health effects data.

❑ Use of probabilistic approaches for ERA.

☐ Integrating probabilistic exposure and risk estimates and communicating uncertainty and variability.

In order to support the development of guidance on these or related topics, following studies or research are recommended:

☐ The use of PRA models to evaluate toxicity data has been very limited. Scientific, technical and policy-based discussions are needed in this area.

☐ Additional research on formal methods for treating model uncertainties will be valuable.

Some steps to improve implementation include these:

☐ Informing decision makers about the advantages and disadvantages of using PRA techniques in their decision-making processes through lectures, webinars and communications regarding the techniques and their use in EPA.

☐ Incorporating a discussion of PRA tools during Planning and Scoping for HHRAs and ERAs.

☐ Continuing the dialogue between assessors and managers on how to use PRA within the regulatory decision making process.

☐ Conducting meetings and discussions of PRA techniques and their application with both managers and assessors to aid in providing greater consistency and transparency in EPA's risk assessment and risk management process and in developing EPA's internal capacity.

☐ Developing a "Community of Practice" for further discussion regarding the application of PRA techniques and the use of these tools in decision making.

Risk assessors and risk managers need information and training so that they can better utilize these tools. Education and experience will generate familiarity with these tools, which will help analysts and decision makers better understand and consider more fully utilizing these techniques within their regulatory programs. Increased training is needed to facilitate understanding on all levels and may include the following:

☐ Providing introductory as well as advanced training to all EPA offices.

☐ Training risk assessors and risk managers in the PRA techniques so that they can learn about the various tools available, their applications, software and review considerations, and resources for additional information (e.g., experts and support services within the Agency).

☐ Providing easily available, flexible, modular training for all levels of experience to familiarize EPA employees with the menu of tools and their capacities.

☐ Providing live and recorded seminars and webinars for introductory and supplemental education, as well as periodic, centralized hands-on training sessions demonstrating how to utilize software programs.

Training is critical both for an improved understanding but also to build increased capacity in the Agency and explicit steps could include these:

☐ Demonstrating, through informational opportunities and resource libraries, the various tools and methods that can be used at all stages of risk analysis to aid the decision-making process by characterizing inter-individual variability and uncertainties.

☐ Promoting the sharing of experience, knowledge, models and best practices via meetings of risk assessors and managers; electronic exchanges, such as the EPA Portal Environmental

Science Connector (https://ssoprod.epa.gov/sso/jsp/obloginESCNew.jsp); and more detailed discussions of the case studies.

As EPA works toward the more integrated evaluation of environmental problems, this will include not just the improved understanding of single pollutants/single media, but multi-pollutant, multi-media and multi-receptor analysis within a decision analytic framework. EPA is beginning to build such integrated capability into analytical tools like PRA (Babendreier and Castleton 2005; Stahl *et al.* 2011).

The RAF will be taking a leadership role through the Uncertainty and Variability Workgroup to more fully evaluate the application and use of PRA tools and broadening the dialogue between assessors and managers. Updates on the progress of this Technical Panel will be provided on the RAF webpage at: www.epa.gov/raf.

GLOSSARY

Analysis. Examination of anything complex to understand its nature or to determine its essential features (WHO 2004).

Assessment. A determination or appraisal of possible consequences resulting from an analysis of data (2011b).

Assessment endpoint. An explicit expression of the environmental value that is to be protected, operationally defined by an ecological entity and its attributes. For example, salmon are valued ecological entities; reproduction and age class structure are some of their important attributes. Together, salmon "reproduction and age class structure" form an assessment endpoint (USEPA 1998b).

Bayesian probability. An approach to probability, representing a personal degree of belief that a value of random variable will be observed. Alternatively, the use of probability measures to characterize the degree of uncertainty (Gelman *et al.* 2004).

Bayesian Analysis. Bayesian analysis is a method of statistical inference in which the knowledge of prior events is used to predict future events (USEPA 2011b).

Correlation. An estimate of the degree to which two sets of variables vary together, with no distinction between dependent and independent variables. Correlation refers to a broad class of statistical relationships involving dependence (USEPA 2012).

Critical control point. A controllable variable that can be adjusted to reduce exposure and risk. For example, a critical control point might be the emission rate from a particular emission source. The concept of critical control point is from the hazard assessment and critical control point concept for risk management that is used in space and food safety applications, among others (USEPA 2006c).

Critical limit. A numerical value of a critical control point at or below which risk is considered to be acceptable. A criterion that separates acceptability from unacceptability (USEPA 2006c).

Deterministic. A methodology relying on point (i.e., exact) values as inputs to estimate risk; this obviates quantitative estimates of uncertainty and variability. Results also are presented as point values. Uncertainty and variability may be discussed qualitatively or semi-quantitatively by multiple deterministic risk estimates (USEPA 2006b).

Deterministic risk assessment (DRA). Risk evaluation involving the calculation and expression of risk as a single numerical value or "single point" estimate of risk, with uncertainty and variability discussed qualitatively (USEPA 2012).

Ecological risk assessment. The process that evaluates the likelihood that adverse ecological effects may occur or are occurring as a result of exposure to one or more stressors (USEPA 1998b).

Ecosystem. The biotic community and abiotic environment within a specified location in space and time (USEPA 1998b).

Ensemble. A method for predictive modeling based on multiple measures of the same event over time (e.g., the amount of carbon dioxide present in the atmosphere at selected time points). The collection of data input is known as an ensemble and can be used to develop a quantification of prediction variability within the model. Ensemble modeling is used most commonly in atmospheric prediction in forecasting, although ensemble modeling has been applied to biological systems to better quantify risks of events or perturbations within biological systems (Fuentes and Foley 2012).

Environment. The sum of all external conditions affecting the life, development and survival of an organism (USEPA 2010a).

Expert elicitation. A systematic process of formalizing and quantifying, typically in probabilistic terms, expert judgments about uncertain quantities (USEPA 2011a).

Frequentist (or frequency) probability. A view of probability that concerns itself with the frequency with which an event occurs given a long sequence of identical and independent trials (USEPA 1997b).

Hazard identification. The risk assessment process of determining whether exposure to a stressor can cause an increase in the incidence or severity of a particular adverse effect, and whether an adverse effect is likely to occur (USEPA 2012).

Human health risk assessment. 1. The process to estimate the nature and probability of adverse health effects in humans who may be exposed to chemicals in contaminated environmental media, now or in the future (USEPA 2010b). 2. The evaluation of scientific information on the hazardous properties of environmental agents (hazard characterization), the dose-response relationship (dose-response assessment), and the extent of human exposure to those agents (exposure assessment). The product of the risk assessment is a statement regarding the probability that populations or individuals so exposed will be harmed and to what degree (risk characterization) (USEPA 2006a).

Inputs. Quantities that are applied to a model (WHO 2008).

Likelihood Function. An approach to modeling exposure in which long-term exposure of an individual is simulated as the sum of separate short-term exposure events (USEPA 2001).

Microenvironment. Well-defined surroundings such as the home, office, automobile, kitchen, store, etc., that can be treated as homogenous (or well characterized) in the concentrations of a chemical or other agent (USEPA 1992).

Microexposure event (MEE) analysis. An approach to modeling exposure in which long-term exposure of an individual is simulated as the sum of separate short-term exposure events (USEPA 2001).

Model. A mathematical representation of a natural system intended to mimic the behavior of the real system, allowing description of empirical data, and predictions about untested states of the system (USEPA 2006b).

Model boundaries. 1. Decisions regarding the time, space, number of chemicals, etc., used in guiding modeling of the system. Risks can be understated or overstated if the model boundary is mis-specified. For example, if a study area is defined to be too large and includes a significant number of low-exposure areas, then a population-level risk distribution can be diluted by including less exposed individuals, which can, in turn, result in a risk-based decision that does not protect sufficiently the most exposed individuals in the study area. 2. Designated areas of competence of the model, including time, space, pathogens, pathways, exposed populations, and acceptable ranges of values for each input and jointly among all inputs for which the model meets data quality objectives (WHO 2008).

Modeling. Development of a mathematical or physical representation of a system or theory that accounts for all or some of its known properties. Models often are used to test the effect of changes of components on the overall performance of the system (USEPA 2010a).

Model uncertainty (sources of):

❑ *Model structure. A set of assumptions and inference options upon which a model is based, including underlying theory as well as specific functional relationships (WHO 2008).*

☐ **Model detail.** *Level of simplicity or detail associated with the functional relationships assumed in the model compared to the actual but unknown relationships in the system being modeled (WHO 2008).*

☐ **Extrapolation.** *Use of models outside of the parameter space used in their derivation may result in erroneous predictions. For example, a threshold for health effects may exist at exposure levels below those covered by a particular epidemiological study. If that study is used in modeling health effects at those lower levels (and it is assumed that the level of response seen in the study holds for lower levels of exposure), then disease incidence may be overestimated (USEPA 2007a).*

Monte Carlo analysis (MCA) or simulation (MCS). A repeated random sampling from the distribution of values for each of the parameters in a generic exposure or risk equation to derive an estimate of the distribution of exposures or risks in the population (USEPA 2006b).

One-dimensional Monte Carlo analysis (1-D MCA). A numerical method of simulating a distribution for an endpoint of concern as a function of probability distributions that characterize variability or uncertainty. Distributions used to characterize variability are distinguished from distributions used to characterize uncertainty (WHO 2008).

Parameter. A quantity used to calibrate or specify a model, such as 'parameters' of a probability model (e.g., mean and standard deviation for a normal distribution). Parameter values often are selected by fitting a model to a calibration data set (WHO 2008).

Probability. A frequentist approach considers the frequency with which samples are obtained within a specified range or for a specified category (e.g., the probability that an average individual with a particular mean dose will develop an illness) (WHO 2008).

Probabilistic risk analysis (PRA). Calculation and expression of health risks using multiple risk descriptors to provide the likelihood of various risk levels. Probabilistic risk results approximate a full range of possible outcomes and the likelihood of each, which often is presented as a frequency distribution graph, thus allowing uncertainty or variability to be expressed quantitatively (USEPA 2012).

Problem formulation. The initial stage of a risk assessment where the purpose of the assessment is articulated, exposure and risk scenarios are considered, a conceptual model is developed, and a plan for analyzing and characterizing risk is determined (USEPA 2004a).

Reference concentration (RfC). An estimate (with uncertainty spanning approximately an order of magnitude) of a continuous inhalation exposure to the human population (including sensitive subgroups) that is likely to be without an appreciable risk of deleterious effects during a lifetime. It can be derived from a No-Observed-Adverse-Effect Level (NOAEL), Lowest-Observed-Adverse-Effect Level (LOAEL), or benchmark concentration, with uncertainty factors generally applied to reflect limitations of the data used. It is generally used in EPA's noncancer health assessments (USEPA 2007a).

Reference dose (RfD). An estimate (with uncertainty spanning approximately an order of magnitude) of a daily oral exposure to the human population (including sensitive subgroups) that is likely to be without an appreciable risk of deleterious effects during a lifetime. It can be derived from a NOAEL, LOAEL or benchmark dose, with uncertainty factors generally applied to reflect limitations of the data used. It is typically used in EPA's noncancer health assessments (USEPA 2011c).

Risk. 1. Risk includes consideration of exposure to the possibility of an adverse outcome, the frequency with which one or more types of adverse outcomes may occur, and the severity or consequences of the adverse outcomes if such occur. 2. The potential for realization of unwanted, adverse consequences to human life, health, property or the environment. 3. The probability of adverse effects resulting from exposure to an environmental agent or mixture of agents. 4. The combined answers to: What can go wrong? How likely is it? What are the consequences? (USEPA 2011c).

Risk analysis. A process for identifying, characterizing, controlling and communicating risks in situations where an organism, system, subpopulation or population could be exposed to a hazard. Risk analysis is a process that includes risk assessment, risk management and risk communication (WHO 2008).

Risk assessment. 1. A process intended to calculate or estimate the risk to a given target organism, system, subpopulation or population, including the identification of attendant uncertainties following exposure to a particular agent, taking into account the inherent characteristics of the agent of concern, as well as the characteristics of the specific target system (WHO 2008). 2. The evaluation of scientific information on the hazardous properties of environmental agents (hazard characterization), the dose-response relationship (dose-response assessment), and the extent of human exposure to those agents (exposure assessment) (NRC 1983). The product of the risk assessment is a statement regarding the probability that populations or individuals so exposed will be harmed and to what degree (risk characterization; USEPA 2000a). 3. Qualitative and quantitative evaluation of the risk posed to human health or the environment by the actual or potential presence or use of specific pollutants (USEPA 2012).

Risk-based decision making. A process through which decisions are made according to the risk each posed to human health and the environment (USEPA 2012).

Risk management. A decision-making process that takes into account environmental laws; regulations; and political, social, economic, engineering and scientific information, including a risk assessment, to weigh policy alternatives associated with a hazard (USEPA 2011c).

Scenario. A set of facts, assumptions and inferences about how exposure takes place that aids the exposure assessor in evaluating, estimating or quantifying exposures (USEPA 1992). Scenarios might include identification of pollutants, pathways, exposure routes and modes of action, among others.

Sensitivity analysis. The process of changing one variable while leaving the others constant to determine its effect on the output. This procedure fixes each uncertain quantity at its credible lower and upper bounds (holding all others at their nominal values, such as medians) and computes the results of each combination of values. The results help to identify the variables that have the greatest effect on exposure estimates and help focus further information-gathering efforts (USEPA 2011b).

Tiered approach. Refers to various hierarchical tiers (levels) of complexity and refinement for different types of modeling approaches that can be used in risk assessment. A deterministic risk assessment with conservative assumptions is an example of a lower level type of analysis (Tier 0) that can be used to determine whether exposures and risks are below levels of concern. Examples of progressively higher levels include the use of deterministic risk assessment coupled with sensitivity analysis (Tier 1), the use of probabilistic techniques to characterize either variability or uncertainty only (Tier 2), and the use of two-dimensional probabilistic techniques to distinguish between but simultaneously characterize both variability and uncertainty (Tier 3) (USEPA 2004a and WHO 2008).

Two-dimensional Monte Carlo analysis (2-D MCA). An advanced numerical modeling technique that uses two stages of random sampling, also called nested loops, to distinguish between variability and uncertainty in exposure and toxicity variables. The first stage, often called the inner loop, involves a complete 1-D MCA simulation of variability in risk. In the second stage, often called the outer loop, parameters of the probability distributions are redefined to reflect uncertainty. These loops are repeated many times resulting in multiple risk distributions, from which confidence intervals are calculated to represent uncertainty in the population distribution of risk (WHO 2008).

Uncertainty. Uncertainty occurs because of a lack of knowledge. It is not the same as variability. For example, a risk assessor may be very certain that different people drink different amounts of water but may be uncertain about how much variability there is in water intakes within the population. Uncertainty often can be reduced by collecting more and better data, whereas variability is an inherent property of the population being evaluated. Variability can be better characterized with more data but it cannot be reduced or eliminated. Efforts to clearly distinguish between variability and uncertainty are important for both risk assessment and risk characterization, although they both may be incorporated into an assessment (USEPA 2011c).

Uncertainty analysis. A detailed examination of the systematic and random errors of a measurement or estimate; an analytical process to provide information regarding uncertainty (USEPA 2006b).

Value of information. An analysis that involves estimating the value that new information can have to a risk manager before the information is actually obtained. It is a measure of the importance of uncertainty in terms of the expected improvement in a risk management decision that might come from better information (USEPA 2001).

Variability. Refers to true heterogeneity or diversity, as exemplified in natural variation. For example, among a population that drinks water from the same source and with the same contaminant concentration, the risks from consuming the water may vary. This may result from differences in exposure (e.g., different people drinking different amounts of water and having different body weights, exposure frequencies and exposure durations), as well as differences in response (e.g., genetic differences in resistance to a chemical dose). Those inherent differences are referred to as variability. Differences among individuals in a population are referred to as inter-individual variability, and differences for one individual over time are referred to as intra-individual variability (USEPA 2011c).

REFERENCES

Ang, A. H-S., and W. H. Tang. 1984. *Probability Concepts in Engineering Planning and Design, Volume 2: Decision, Risk, and Reliability.* New York: John Wiley & Sons.

Babendreier, J. E., and K. J. Castleton. 2005. "Investigating Uncertainty and Sensitivity in Integrated, Multimedia Environmental Models: Tools for FRAMES-3MRA." *Environmental Modeling & Software* 20: 1043–1055.

Bloom, D. L., D. M. Byrne, and J. M. Andreson. 1993. *Communicating Risk to Senior EPA Policy-Makers: A Focus Group Study.* Prepared by Bloom Research and the Office of Air Quality Planning and Standards. Research Triangle Park, NC: USEPA.

Burnham, K. P., and D. R. Anderson. 2002. *Model Selection and Inference: A Practical Information-Theoretic Approach.* 2nd ed. New York: Springer-Verlag.

Clyde, M., P. Guttorp, and E. Sullivan. 2000. *Effects of Ambient Fine and Coarse Particles on Mortality in Phoenix, Arizona.* National Research Center for Statistics and the Environment Technical Report Series, No. 40.

Cooke, R. M. 1991. *Experts in Uncertainty: Opinion and Subjective Probability in Science.* New York: Oxford University Press.

Costanza, R., S. O. Funtowicz, and J. R. Ravetz. 1997. "Assessing and Communicating Data Quality in Policy-Relevant Research." In *Frontiers in Ecological Economics: Transdisciplinary Essays,* by Robert Costanza, 283–308. Cheltenham, UK: E. Elgar.

Cullen, A. C., and H. C. Frey. 1999. *Probabilistic Exposure Assessment: A Handbook for Dealing with Variability and Uncertainty in Models and Inputs.* New York: Plenum Press.

Evans, J. S., J. D. Graham, G. M. Gray, and R. L. Sielken. 1994. "A Distributional Approach to Characterizing Low-Dose Cancer Risk." *Risk Analysis* 14 (1): 25–34.

Ferson, S., R. Nelsen, J. Hajagos, D. Berleant, J. Zhang, W. T. Tucker, L. Ginzburg, and W. L. Oberkampf. 2004. *Dependence in Probabilistic Modeling, Dempster-Shafer Theory, and Probability Bounds Analysis.* SAND20043072. Albuquerque, NM: Sandia National Laboratories. www.ramas.com/depend.pdf.

Ferson, S., W. L. Oberkampt, and L. Ginzburg. 2009. "Validation of Imprecise Probability Models." *International Journal of Reliability and Safety* 3 (1–3): 3–22.

Finkel, A. M. 1989. "Is Risk Assessment Really Too Conservative?: Revising the Revisionists." *Journal of Environmental Law* 14: 427–67.

Fisher, L., P. Pascual, and W. Wagner. 2006. *Mapping the Role of Models in U.S. and E.U. Risk Regulation: A Legal Background Paper.* Washington, D.C.: The Association of Union Constructors Workshop.

Fischhoff, B. 1995. "Ranking Risks." *Risk: Health, Safety & Environment* 6: 191–202.

Frey, H. C., and S. R. Patil. 2002. "Identification and Review of Sensitivity Analysis Methods." *Risk Analysis* 22 (3): 553–78.

Fuentes, M. and K. Foley. 2012. "Ensemble Models." In Abdel, H. and Walter W. El-Shaarawai (eds.) *Encyclopedia of Environmetrics.* Indianapolis: John Wiley and Sons.

Gelman, A., J. B. Carlin, H. S. Stern, and D. B. Rubin. 2004. *Bayesian Data Analysis.* 2nd ed. Boca Raton, FL: Chapman and Hall/CRC.

Hattis, D., S. Baird, and R. Goble. 2002. "A Straw Man Proposal for a Quantitative Definition of the RfD." *Drug and Chemical Toxicology* 25 (4): 403–36.

Hattis, D. B., and D. E. Burmaster. 1994. "Assessment of Variability and Uncertainty Distributions for Practical Risk Analyses." *Risk Analysis* 14 (5): 713–30.

Hattis, D., and M. K. Lynch. 2010. *Alternatives to Pollutant-by-Pollutant Dose-Response Estimation for Air Toxics (Final Report).* EPA-W-05-022, WA 3-80. Washington, D.C.: USEPA.

Hoeting, J. A., D. Madigan, A. E. Raftery, and C. T. Volinsky. 1999. "Bayesian Model Averaging: A Tutorial." *Statistical Science* 14 (4): 382–417.

IEC (Industrial Economics, Inc.). 2006. *Expanded Expert Judgment Assessment of the Concentration-Response Relationship Between PM$_{2.5}$ Exposure and Mortality (Final Report).* Research Triangle Park, NC: USEPA. http://www.epa.gov/ttn/ecas/regdata/Uncertainty/pm_ee_report.pdf.

Institute of Medicine. 2013. *Environmental Decisions in the Face of Uncertainty.* Washington, D.C.: The National Academies Press.

Illing, H. P. A. 1999. "Are Societal Judgments Being Incorporated Into the Uncertainty Factors Used in Toxicological Risk Assessment?" *Regulatory Toxicology and Pharmacology* 29 (3): 300–308.

Krupnick, A., R. Morgenstern, M. Batz, P. Nelson, D. Burtraw, J. Shih, and M. McWilliams. 2006. *Not a Sure Thing: Making Regulatory Choices Under Uncertainty.* Washington, D.C.: Resources for the Future. http://www.rff.org/rff/Documents/RFF-Rpt-RegulatoryChoices.pdf.

Kunreuther, H. C., and P. Slovic. 1996. "Science, Values and Risk." *Annals of the American Academy of Political and Social Science* 545: 116–25.

Lester, R. R., L. C. Green, and I. Linkov. 2007. "Site-Specific Applications of Probabilistic Health Risk Assessment: Review of the Literature Since 2000." *Risk Analysis* 27: 635–58.

McConnell, K. E. 1997. "Using Cost-Benefit Analysis in the Management of Contaminated Sediments (Appendix E)." In *Contaminated Sediments in Ports and Waterways: Cleanup Strategies and Technologies,* by the Commission on Engineering and Technical Systems of the National Research Council, 239–56. Washington, D.C.: The National Academies Press.

Mokhtari, A., H. C. Frey, and J. Zheng. 2006. "Evaluation and Recommendation of Sensitivity Analysis Methods for Application to Stochastic Human Exposure and Dose Simulation (SHEDS) Models." *Journal of Exposure Science and Environmental Epidemiology* 16 (6): 491–506.

Morgan, G., H. Dowlatabadi, M. Henrion, D. Keith, R. Lempert, S. McBrid, M. Small, and T. Wilbanks, eds. 2009. *Best Practice Approaches for Characterizing, Communicating, and Incorporating Scientific Uncertainty in Decision Making.* Final Report. Washington, D.C.: U.S. Climate Change Science Program, National Oceanic and Atmospheric Administration. http://library.globalchange.gov/sap-5-2-best-practice-approaches-for-characterizing-communicating-and-incorporating-scientific-uncertainty-in-decisionmaking.

Morgan, M. G., and M. Henrion. 1990. *Uncertainty: A Guide to Dealing with Uncertainty in Quantitative Risk and Policy Analysis.* New York: Cambridge University Press.

NRC (National Research Council). 1983. *Risk Assessment in the Federal Government: Managing the Process.* Committee on the Institutional Means for Assessment of Risks to Public Health. Washington, D.C.: The National Academies Press.

NRC. 1989. *Risk Assessment in the Federal Government: Managing the Process.* Washington, D.C.: The National Academies Press.

NRC. 1991. *Rethinking the Ozone Problem in Urban and Regional Air Pollution.* Washington, D.C.: The National Academies Press.

NRC. 1993. *Issues in Risk Assessment.* Washington, D.C.: The National Academies Press.

NRC. 1994. *Science and Judgment in Risk Assessment.* Washington, D.C.: The National Academies Press.

NRC. 2002. *Estimating the Public Health Benefits of Proposed Air Pollution Regulations.* Washington, D.C.: The National Academies Press.

NRC. 2007a. *Scientific Review of the Proposed Risk Assessment Bulletin From the Office of Management and Budget.* Washington, D.C.: The National Academies Press.

NRC. 2007b. *Models in Environmental Regulatory Decision Making.* Washington, D.C.: The National Academies Press.

NRC. 2009. *Science and Decisions: Advancing Risk Assessment.* Washington, D.C.: The National Academies Press.

OSTP (Office of Science and Technology Policy)/OMB (Office of Management and Budget). 2007. Memorandum (M-07-24) for the Heads of Executive Departments and Agencies; from Susan E. Dudley, Administrator, Office of Information and Regulatory Affairs, Office of Management and Budget, to Sharon L. Hays, Associate Director and Deputy Director for Science, Office of Science and Technology Policy: Updated Principles for Risk Analysis. September 19, 2007.

Özkaynak H., H.C. Frey, J. Burke, and R.W. Pinder. 2009. "Analysis of Coupled Model Uncertainties in Source-to-Dose Modeling of Human Exposures to Ambient Air Pollution: A $PM_{2.5}$ Case-Study." *Atmospheric Environment* 43: 1641–49.

Parkin, R. T., and M. G. Morgan. 2007. *Consultation on Enhancing Risk Assessment Practices and Updating EPA's Exposure Guidelines.* EPA/SAB-07/003. Washington, D.C.: USEPA. USEPA. 2007. Letter From M. G. Morgan and R. T. Parkin, Science Advisory Board, to S. Johnson, U.S. Environmental Protection Agency. February 28, 2007. EPA/SAB-07/003. http://yosemite.epa.gov/sab/sabproduct.nsf/55E1B2C78C6085EB8525729C00573A3E/$File/sab-07-003.pdf.

PCCRARM (Presidential/Congressional Commission on Risk Assessment and Risk Management). 1997. *Framework for Environmental Health Risk Management Final Report, Volume 1.* Washington, D.C.: PCCRARM. http://www.riskworld.com/nreports/1997/risk-rpt/pdf/EPAJAN.PDF.

Pearl, J. 2009. *Causality: Models, Reasoning, and Inference.* 2nd ed. New York: Cambridge University Press.

Royall, R. M. 1997. *Statistical Evidence: A Likelihood Paradigm.* London: Chapman & Hall.

Saltelli, A., S. Tarantola, F. Campolongo, and M. Rattoet. 2004. *Sensitivity Analysis in Practice.* New York: John Wiley & Sons.

Stahl, C. H., and A. J. Cimorelli. 2005. "How Much Uncertainty Is Too Much and How Do We Know? A Case Example of the Assessment of Ozone Monitor Network Options." *Risk Analysis* 25 (5): 1109–20.

Stahl, C. H., and A. J. Cimorelli. 2012. "The Demonstration of the Necessity and Feasibility of Using a Clumsy Decision Analytic Approach in Wicked Environmental Problems." *Integrated Environmental Assessment and Management* 9 (1):17.

Stahl, C. H., A. J. Cimorelli, C. Mazzarella, and B. Jenkins. 2011. "Toward Sustainability: A Case Study Demonstrating Transdisciplinary Learning." *Integrated Environmental Assessment and Management* 7 (3): 483–98.

Swartout, J. C., P. S. Price, M. L. Dourson, H. L. Carlson-Lynch, and R. E. Keenan. 1998. "Probabilistic Framework for the Reference Dose (Probabilistic RfD)." *Risk Analysis* 18 (3): 271–82.

Toll, J., S. Pavlou, D. Lee, L. Zaragosa, and P. Shelley. 1997. "Using Decision Analysis in the Management of Contaminated Sediments (Appendix E)." In *Contaminated Sediments in Ports and Waterways: Cleanup Strategies and Technologies,* by the Commission on Engineering and Technical Systems of the National Research Council, 257–84. Washington, D.C.: The National Academies Press.

Toll, J. E. 1999. "Elements of Environmental Problem-Solving." *Human and Ecological Risk Assessment* 5 (2): 275–80.

USEPA (U.S. Environmental Protection Agency). 1992. *Guidelines for Exposure Assessment.* EPA/600/Z-92/001. Washington, D.C.: Risk Assessment Forum, USEPA. http://cfpub.epa.gov/ncea/cfm/recordisplay.cfm?deid=15263.

USEPA. 1995a. *Guidance for Risk Characterization.* Washington, D.C.: Science Policy Council, USEPA. http://www.epa.gov/spc/pdfs/rcguide.pdf.

USEPA. 1995b. *Policy for Risk Characterization.* Washington, D.C.: USEPA. http://www.epa.gov/oswer/riskassessment/pdf/1995_0521_risk_characterization_program.pdf.

USEPA. 1997a. *Policy for Use of Probabilistic Analysis in Risk Assessment at the U.S. Environmental Protection Agency.* Washington, D.C.: USEPA. http://www.epa.gov/spc/pdfs/probpol.pdf.

USEPA. 1997b. *Guiding Principles for Monte Carlo Analysis.* EPA/630/R-97/001. Washington, D.C.: USEPA. http://www.epa.gov/raf/publications/pdfs/montecar.pdf.

USEPA. 1998a. *Guidance for Submission of Probabilistic Human Health Exposure Assessments to the Office of Pesticide Programs (Draft).* Washington, D.C.: USEPA. http://www.epa.gov/fedrgstr/EPA-PEST/1998/November/Day-05/6021.pdf.

USEPA. 1998b. *Guidelines for Ecological Risk Assessment.* EPA/630/R-95/002F. Washington, D.C.: Risk Assessment Forum, USEPA. http://www.epa.gov/raf/publications/pdfs/ECOTXTBX.PDF.

USEPA. 2000a. *EPA Science Policy Council Handbook: Risk Characterization.* EPA/100/B-00/002. Washington, D.C.: USEPA. http://www.epa.gov/spc/pdfs/rchandbk.pdf.

USEPA. 2000b. *Toward Integrating Environmental Decision-Making.* EPA/SAB/EC-00/011. Washington, D.C.: Science Advisory Board, USEPA.

USEPA. 2001. *Risk Assessment Guidance for Superfund: Volume III—Part A, Process for Conducting Probabilistic Risk Assessment.* EPA/540/R-02/002. Washington, D.C.: USEPA. http://www.epa.gov/oswer/riskassessment/rags3adt/pdf/rags3adt_complete.pdf.

USEPA. 2004a. *Air Toxics Risk Assessment Reference Library. Volume I: Technical Resource Manual.* EPA/453/K-04/001A. Research Triangle Park, NC: USEPA. http://www.epa.gov/ttn/fera/data/risk/vol_1/title_page_volume_1.pdf.

USEPA. 2004b. *An Examination of EPA Risk Assessment Principles and Practices.* EPA/100/B-04/001. Washington, D.C.: USEPA. http://www.epa.gov/osa/pdfs/ratf-final.pdf.

USEPA. 2006a. *A Framework for Assessing Health Risks of Environmental Exposures to Children.* EPA/600/R-05/093F. Washington, D.C.: USEPA. http://ofmpub.epa.gov/eims/eimscomm.getfile?p_download_id=459047.

USEPA. 2006b. *Air Toxics Risk Assessment Reference Library, Volume 3: Community-Scale Assessment.* EPA/452/K-06/001C. Washington, D.C.: USEPA. http://www.epa.gov/ttn/fera/risk_atra_vol3.html.

USEPA. 2006c. *Hazard Analysis Critical Control Point Strategies for Distribution System Monitoring, Hazard Assessment and Control.* Washington, D.C.: USEPA. http://www.epa.gov/ogwdw/disinfection/tcr/pdfs/issuepaper_tcr_haccp-strategies.pdf.

USEPA. 2007a. *Concepts, Methods and Data Sources for Cumulative Health Risk Assessment of Multiple Chemicals, Exposures and Effects: A Resource Document.* EPA/600/R-06/013F. Washington, D.C.: USEPA. http://cfpub.epa.gov/ncea/risk/recordisplay.cfm?deid=190187.

USEPA. 2007b. Letter From M. G. Morgan and R. T. Parkin, Science Advisory Board, to S. Johnson, U.S. Environmental Protection Agency. February 28, 2007. EPA/SAB-07/003. http://yosemite.epa.gov/sab/sabproduct.nsf/55E1B2C78C6085EB8525729C00573A3E/$File/sab-07-003.pdf.

USEPA. 2010a. *Environmental Monitoring and Assessment Program Master Glossary.* Last modified November 8. http://www.epa.gov/emap

2/html/pubs/docs/resdocs/mglossary.html#ee.

USEPA. 2010b. *Human Health Risk Assessment Onondaga Lake, Lake Bottom Subsite: Sediment Consolidation Area, Camillus, NY.* Washington, D.C.: USEPA. http://www.epa.gov/region2/superfund/npl/onondagalake/healthriskassess.pdf.

USEPA. 2011a. *Expert Elicitation Task Force White Paper.* Washington, D.C.: USEPA. http://www.epa.gov/stpc/pdfs/ee-white-paper-final.pdf.

USEPA. 2011b. *Exposure Factors Handbook: 2011 Edition.* EPA/600/R-09/052F. Washington, D.C.: National Center for Environmental Assessment, Office of Research and Development, USEPA. http://cfpub.epa.gov/ncea/risk/recordisplay.cfm?deid=236252.

USEPA. 2011c. *Integrated Risk Information System Glossary.* Last modified August 21. http://ofmpub.epa.gov/sor_internet/registry/termreg/searchandretrieve/glossariesandkeywordlists/search.do?details=&glossaryName=IRIS%20Glossary.

USEPA. 2012. *Waste and Cleanup Risk Assessment Glossary.* Office of Solid Waste and Emergency Response, USEPA. Last modified December 24. http://www.epa.gov/oswer/riskassessment/glossary.htm.

USEPA. 2014a. *Probabilistic Risk Assessment to Inform Decision Making: Frequently Asked Questions.* EPA/100/R-09/001B. Washington, D.C.: Risk Assessment Forum, Office of the Science Advisor, USEPA.

USEPA. 2014b. *Framework for Human Health Risk Assessment to Inform Decision Making.* EPA/100/R-14/001. Washington, D.C.: Risk Assessment Forum, Office of the Science Advisor, USEPA.

Wilson, J. D. 2000. "Risk Management Cannot Abide Uncertainty." In J. H. Exner and M. L. Trehy (eds.) Symposia papers presented before the Division of Environmental Chemistry, American Chemical Society, August 20–24, 2000. *Preprints of Extended Abstracts* 40 (2): 268–69. Washington, D.C.: American Chemical Society.

WHO (World Health Organization). 2004. *International Programme on Chemical Safety Risk Assessment Terminology.* Geneva: WHO. http://www.who.int/ipcs/methods/harmonization/areas/ipcsterminologyparts1and2.pdf.

WHO. 2008. *Uncertainty and Data Quality in Exposure Assessment.* Geneva: WHO. http://www.who.int/ipcs/publications/methods/harmonization/exposure_assessment.pdf.

Wright, G., F. Bolger, and G. Rowe. 2002. "An Empirical Test of the Relative Validity of Expert and Lay Judgments of Risk." *Risk Analysis* 22 (6): 1107–22.

BIBLIOGRAPHY

Probabilistic Risk Analysis Methodology—General

Cullen, A. C., and H. C. Frey. 1999. *The Use of Probabilistic Techniques in Exposure Assessment: A Handbook for Dealing with Variability and Uncertainty in Models and Inputs.* New York: Plenum.

Dakins, M. E., J. E. Toll, M. J. Small, and K. P. Brand. 1996. "Risk-Based Environmental Remediation: Bayesian Monte Carlo Analysis and the Expected Value of Sample Information." *Risk Analysis* 16 (1): 67–79.

Ferson, S., and V. Kreinovich. 2006. *Modeling Correlation and Dependence Among Intervals.* University of Texas at El Paso Departmental Technical Reports (CS), Paper 131. http://digitalcommons.utep.edu/cs_techrep/131.

Finkel, A. M. 1990. *Confronting Uncertainty in Risk Management: A Guide for Decision-Makers.* Washington, D.C.: Resources for the Future.

Frey, H. C., D. Crawford-Brown, J. Zheng, and D. Loughlin. 2003. *Hierarchy of Methods to Characterize Uncertainty: State of Science of Methods for Describing and Quantifying Uncertainty (Draft).* Research Triangle Park, NC: USEPA.

Frey, C., J. Penman, L. Hanle, S. Monni, and S. Ogle. 2006. Chapter 3, "Uncertainties." In S. Eggleston, L. Buendia, K. Miwa, T. Ngara, and K. Tanabe (eds.) *2006 IPCC Guidelines for National Greenhouse Gas Inventories, Volume I: General Guidance and Reporting.* Kanagawa, Japan: National Greenhouse Gas Inventories Programme, Inter-Governmental Panel on Climate Change.

Hattis, D. 1996. "Human Interindividual Variability in Susceptibility to Toxic Effects—From Annoying Detail to a Central Determinant of Risk." *Toxicology* 111: 5–14.

Hattis, D., and E. Anderson. 1999. "What Should Be the Implications of Uncertainty, Variability, and Inherent 'Biases'/'Conservatism' for Risk Management Decision Making?" *Risk Analysis* 19: 95–107.

Hattis, D., and M. K. Lynch. 2007. "Empirically Observed Distributions of Pharmacokinetic and Pharmacodynamic Variability in Humans—Implications for the Derivation of Single Point Component Uncertainty Factors Providing Equivalent Protection as Existing RfDs." In J. C. Lipscomb and E. V. Ohanian (eds.) *Toxicokinetics in Risk Assessment,* 69–93. New York: Informa Healthcare USA, Inc.

Hattis, D. 2009. "Failure to Communicate—Comment: Regulator/Risk Perspective on Burzala and Mazzuchi's Paper." In R.M. Cooke (ed.). *Uncertainty Modeling in Dose Response: Bench Testing Environmental Toxicity,* 153–59. New York: John Wiley & Sons, Inc.

Loughlin, D., H. C. Frey, K. Hanisak, and A. Eyth. 2003. *Implementation Requirements for the Development of a Sensitivity/Uncertainty Analysis Tool for MIMS (Draft).* Research Triangle Park, NC: USEPA.

Morgan, M. G., and M. Henrion. 1990. *Uncertainty: A Guide to Dealing with Uncertainty in Quantitative Risk and Policy Analysis.* New York: Cambridge University Press.

NARSTO (North American Research Strategy for Tropospheric Ozone). 2005. *Improving Emission Inventories for Effective Air Quality Management Across North America, A NARSTO Assessment.* NARSTO-05-001. Pasco, WA: NARSTO.

NRC (National Research Council). 1994. *Science and Judgment in Risk Assessment.* Washington, D.C.: The National Academies Press.

USEPA (U.S. Environmental Protection Agency). 1997. *Guiding Principles for Monte Carlo Analysis.* EPA/630/R-97/001. Washington, D.C.: USEPA. http://www.epa.gov/raf/publications/pdfs/montecar.pdf.

Probabilistic Risk Analysis and Decision Making

Bernardini, A., and F. Tonon. 2010. *Bounding Uncertainty in Civil Engineering: Theoretical Background.* New York: Springer.

Bloom, D. L., D. M. Byrne, and J. M. Andreson. 1993. *Communicating Risk to Senior EPA Policy-Makers: A Focus Group Study.* Research Triangle Park, NC: USEPA.

Krupnick, A., R. Morgenstern, M. Batz, P. Nelson, D. Burtraw, J.-S. Shih, and M. McWilliams. 2006. *Not a Sure Thing: Making Regulatory Choices Under Uncertainty.* Washington, D.C.: Resources for the Future.

McGarity, T. O., and W. E. Wagner. 2003. "Legal Aspects of the Regulatory Use of Environmental Modeling." *Environmental Law Reporter* 33: 10751–74.

NRC. 1996. *Understanding Risk: Informing Decisions in a Democratic Society.* Washington, D.C.: The National Academies Press.

NRC. 2009. *Science and Decisions: Advancing Risk Assessment.* Washington, D.C.: The National Academies Press.

Pascual, P., N. Steiber, and E. Sunderland. 2003. *Draft Guidance on the Development, Evaluation, and Application of Regulatory Environmental Models.* Washington, D.C.: USEPA.

Thompson, K. M., and J. D. Graham. 1996. "Going Beyond the Single Number: Using Probabilistic Risk Assessment to Improve Risk Management." *Human and Ecological Risk Assessment* 2 (4): 1008–34.

USEPA. 1997. Memo from Fred Hansen. *Use of Probabilistic Techniques (including Monte Carlo Analysis) in Risk Assessment,* dated May 15, 1997. Washington, D.C.: USEPA.

Vick, S. G. 2002. *Degrees of Belief: Subjective Probability and Engineering Judgment.* Reston, VA: ASCE Press.

Probabilistic Risk Analysis Methodology—Specific Aspects

Abdel-Aziz, A., and H. C. Frey. 2003. "Development of Hourly Probabilistic Utility NO_x Emission Inventories Using Time Series Techniques: Part I—Univariate Approach." *Atmospheric Environment* 37: 5379–89.

Abdel-Aziz, A., and H.C. Frey. 2003. "Development of Hourly Probabilistic Utility NO_x Emission Inventories Using Time Series Techniques: Part II—Multivariate Approach." *Atmospheric Environment* 37: 5391–401.

Abdel-Aziz, A., and H. C. Frey. 2004. "Propagation of Uncertainty in Hourly Utility NO_x Emissions Through a Photochemical Grid Air Quality Model: A Case Study for the Charlotte, NC Modeling Domain." *Environmental Science & Technology* 38 (7): 2153–60.

Casman, E. A., M. G. Morgan, and H. Dowlatabadi. 1999. "Mixed Levels of Uncertainty in Complex Policy Models." *Risk Analysis* 19 (1): 33–42.

Crawford-Brown, D. J., and K. G. Brown. 1987. "A Framework for Assessing the Rationality of Judgments in Carcinogenicity Hazard Identification." *Risk: Health, Safety and Environment* 8: 307–37.

Draper, D. 1995. "Assessment and Propagation of Model Uncertainty." *Journal of the Royal Statistical Society* 57: 45–97.

Evans, J. S., J. D. Graham, G. M. Gray, and R. L. Sielken. 1994. "A Distributional Approach to Characterizing Low-Dose Cancer Risk." *Risk Analysis* 14 (1): 25–34.

Frey, H. C., and D. E. Burmaster. 1999. "Methods for Characterizing Variability and Uncertainty: Comparison of Bootstrap Simulation and Likelihood-Based Approaches." *Risk Analysis* 19 (1): 109–30.

Frey, H. C., and D. S. Rhodes. 1996. "Characterizing, Simulating, and Analyzing Variability and Uncertainty: An Illustration of Methods Using an Air Toxics Emissions Example." *Human and Ecological Risk Assessment: An International Journal* 2 (4): 762–97.

Frey, H. C., and Y. Zhao. 2004. "Quantification of Variability and Uncertainty for Air Toxic Emission Inventories With Censored Emission Factor Data." *Environmental Science & Technology* 38 (22): 6094–100.

Landis, W. G. 2005. *Regional Scale Ecological Risk Assessment Using the Relative Risk Model.* Boca Raton, FL: CRC Press.

Maginnis, C. M. 2006. *A Screening Level Integrated Ecological and Human Health Risk Assessment for Lake Whatcom, Whatcom County, Washington.* Master's Thesis, Western Washington University.

Shlyakhter, A. I. 1994. "An Improved Framework for Uncertainty Analysis: Accounting for Unsuspected Errors." *Risk Analysis* 14: 441–47.

Zheng, J., and H. C. Frey. 2004. "Quantification of Variability and Uncertainty Using Mixture Distributions: Evaluation of Sample Size, Mixing Weights and Separation between Components." *Risk Analysis* 24 (3): 553–71.

Zheng, J., and H. C. Frey. 2005. "Quantitative Analysis of Variability and Uncertainty with Known Measurement Error: Methodology and Case Study." *Risk Analysis* 25 (3): 663–76.

Sensitivity Analysis

Agro, K. E., C. A. Bradley, and N. Mittmann. 1997. "Sensitivity Analysis in Health Economic and Pharmacoeconomic Studies—an Appraisal of the Literature." *Pharmacoeconomics* 11 (1): 75–88.

Cukier, R.I., H.B. Levine, and K.E. Shuler. 1978. "Nonlinear Sensitivity Analysis of Multi-parameter Model Systems." *Journal of Chemical Physics* 26(1):1–42.

Frey, H. C., and R. Patil. 2002. "Identification and Review of Sensitivity Analysis Methods." *Risk Analysis* 22 (3): 553–77.

Frey, H. C., A. Mokhtari, and J. Zheng. 2004. *Recommended Practice Regarding Selection, Application, and Interpretation of Sensitivity Analysis Methods Applied to Food Safety Process Risk Models.* Washington, D.C.: U.S. Department of Agriculture. http://www.ce.ncsu.edu/risk/Phase3Final.pdf

Helton, J. C., and F. J. Davis. 2002. "Illustration of Sampling-Based Methods for Sensitivity Analysis." *Reliability Engineering & System Safety* 81 (1): 23–69.

Mokhtari, A., and H. C. Frey. 2005. "Recommended Practice Regarding Selection of Sensitivity Analysis Methods Applied to Microbial Food Safety Process Risk Models." *Human and Ecological Risk Assessment* 11 (3): 591–605.

Mokhtari, A., H. C. Frey, and J. Zheng. 2006. "Evaluation and Recommendation of Sensitivity Analysis Methods for Application to EPA-Stochastic Human Exposure and Dose Simulation (SHEDS) Models." *Journal of Exposure Science and Environmental Epidemiology* 16 (6): 491–506.

Saltelli, A., K. Chan, and M. Scott. 2000. *Sensitivity Analysis, Probability and Statistics Series.* New York: John Wiley & Sons.

Sobol, I. M. 1993. "Sensitivity Estimates for Nonlinear Mathematical Models." *Mathematical Modeling and Computation* 1 (4): 407–14.

Xue, J., V. G. Zartarian, H. Özkaynak, W. Dang, G. Glen, L. Smith, and C. Stallings. 2006. "A Probabilistic Arsenic Exposure Assessment for Children Who Contact Chromated Copper Arsenate (CCA)-Treated Playsets and Decks, Part 2: Sensitivity and Uncertainty Analyses." *Risk Analysis* 26 (2): 533–41.

Case Study Examples of Probabilistic Risk Analysis—EPA (See Also the PRA Case Studies Appendix)

Babendreier, J. E., and K. L. Castleton. 2005. "Investigating Uncertainty and Sensitivity in Integrated Multimedia Environmental Models: Tools for FRAMES-3MRA." *Environmental Modeling & Software* 20: 1043–55.

Blancato, J. N., F. W. Power, R. N. Brown, and C. C. Dary. 2006. *Exposure Related Dose Estimating Model (ERDEM): A Physiologically-Based Pharmacokinetic and Pharmacodynamic (PBPK/PD) Model for Assessing Human Exposure and Risk.* EPA/600/R-06/061. Research Triangle Park, NC: USEPA. http://www.epa.gov/heasd/products/erdem/237edrb05-Report.pdf

Burke, J. 2005. *EPA Stochastic Human Exposure and Dose Simulation for Particulate Matter (SHEDS-PM) User's Guide.* Research Triangle Park, NC: USEPA.

Frey, H. C. 2003. *Evaluation of an Approximate Analytical Procedure for Calculating Uncertainty in the Greenhouse Gas Version of the Multi-Scale Motor Vehicle and Equipment Emissions System.* Ann Arbor, MI: USEPA.

Frey, H. C., and Y. Zhao. 2003. *Development of Probabilistic Emission Inventories of Benzene, Formaldehyde and Chromium for the Houston Domain.* Research Triangle Park, NC: USEPA.

Frey, H. C., R. Bharvirkar, and J. Zheng. 1999. *Quantitative Analysis of Variability and Uncertainty in Emissions Estimation.* Research Triangle Park, NC: USEPA.

Frey, H. C., J. Zheng, Y. Zhao, S. Li, and Y. Zhu. 2002. *Technical Documentation of the AuvTool Software for Analysis of Variability and Uncertainty.* Research Triangle Park, NC: USEPA.

Özkaynak H., H. C. Frey, J. Burke, and R. W. Pinder. 2009. "Analysis of Coupled Model Uncertainties in Source-to-Dose Modeling of Human Exposures to Ambient Air Pollution: A $PM_{2.5}$ Case-Study." *Atmospheric Environment* 43: 1641–49.

Zartarian, V. G., J. Xue, H. A. Özkaynak, W. Dang, G. Glen, L. Smith, and C. Stallings. 2005. *A Probabilistic Exposure Assessment for Children Who Contact CCA-Treated Playsets and Decks Using the Stochastic Human Exposure and Dose Simulation Model for the Wood Preservative Scenario (SHEDS-WOOD), Final Report.* EPA/600/X-05/009. Washington, D.C.: USEPA. http://www.epa.gov/heasd/sheds/CCA_all.pdf

Zartarian, V. G., J. Xue, H. Özkaynak, W. Dang, G. Glen, L. Smith, and C. Stallings. 2006. "A Probabilistic Arsenic Exposure Assessment for Children Who Contact CCA-Treated Playsets and Decks, Part 1: Model Methodology, Variability Results, and Model Evaluation." *Risk Analysis* 26 (2): 515–32.

Zheng, J., and H. C. Frey. 2002. *AuvTool User's Guide.* Research Triangle Park, NC: USEPA.

Case Study Examples of Probabilistic Risk Analysis—Other

Bloyd, C., J. Camp, G. Conzelmann, J. Formento, J. Molburg, J. Shannon, M. Henrion, *et al.* 1996. *Tracking and Analysis Framework (TAF) Model Documentation and User's Guide.* ANL/DIS/TM-36. Washington, D.C.: Argonne National Laboratory.

Frey, H. C., and S. Li. 2003. "Quantification of Variability and Uncertainty in AP-42 Emission Factors: Case Studies for Natural Gas-Fueled Engines." *Journal of the Air & Waste Management Association* 53 (12): 1436–47.

Hanna, S. R., Z. Lu, H. C. Frey, N. Wheeler, J. Vukovich, S. Arunachalam, M. Fernau, and D. A. Hansen. 2001. "Uncertainties in Predicted Ozone Concentrations Due to Input Uncertainties for the UAM-V Photochemical Grid Model Applied to the July 1995 OTAG Domain." *Atmospheric Environment* 35 (5): 891–903.

Munns, W. R., Jr., H. A. Walker, and J. F. Paul. 1989. "An Ecological Risk Assessment Framework for Examining the Impacts of Oceanic Disposal Status and Trends Program." In *Oceans '89, Volume 2: Ocean Pollution,* by the Marine Technology Society and the Oceanic Engineering Society (U.S.), 664–69. IEEE Publication No. 89, CH2780-5. New York: IEEE Press.

Munns, W. R., Jr., H. A. Walker, J. F. Paul, and J. H. Gentile. 1996. "A Prospective Assessment of Ecological Risks to Upper Water Column Populations from Ocean Disposal at the 106-Mile Dumpsite." *Journal of Marine Environmental Engineering* 3: 279–97.

Nocito, J. A., H. A. Walker, J. F. Paul, and C. Menzie. 1988. "Application of a Risk Assessment for Marine Disposal of Sewage Sludge at Midshelf and Offshelf Sites." In *Proceedings of the 7th International Ocean Disposal Symposium,* 644–63. Ottawa: Environment Canada.

Nocito, J. A., H. A. Walker, J. F. Paul, and C. A. Menzie. 1989. "Application of a Risk Assessment Framework for Marine Disposal of Sewage Sludge at Midshelf and Offshelf Sites." In G.W. Suter II and M.A. Lewis (eds.). *Aquatic Toxicology and Environmental Fate: Eleventh Volume,* 101–20. ASTM STP 1007. Philadelphia, PA: American Society for Testing and Materials.

Paul, J. F., H. A. Walker, and V. J. Bierman, Jr. 1983. "Probabilistic Approach for the Determination of the Potential Area of Influence for Waste Disposed at the 106-Mile Ocean Disposal Site." In J. B. Pearce, D. C. Miller, and C. Berman (eds.). *106-Mile Waste Disposal Site Characterization Update Report, A–1 to A–8.* NOAA Technical Memorandum NMFS-F/NEC-26. Woods Hole, MA: National Marine Fisheries Service.

Paul, J. F., V. J. Bierman, Jr., W. R. Davis, G. L. Hoffman, W. R. Munns, C. E. Pesch, P. F. Rogerson, and S. C. Schimmel. 1988. "The Application of a Hazard Assessment Research Strategy to the Ocean Disposal of a Dredged Material: Exposure Assessment Component." In D. A. Wolfe and T. P. O'Connor (eds.). *Oceanic Processes in Marine Pollution, Volume 5,* 123–35. Melbourne, FL: Kreiger Publishing Co.

Prager, J. C., V. J. Bierman, Jr., J. F. Paul, and J. S. Bonner. 1986. "Sampling the Oceans for Pollution: A Risk Assessment Approach to Evaluating Low-Level Radioactive Waste Disposal at Sea." *Dangerous Properties of Industrial Materials Report* 6 (3): 2–26.

Walker, H. A., J. F. Paul, J. A. Nocito, and J. H. Gentile. 1988. "Ecological and Human Health Risks for Sewage Sludge Disposal at the 106-Mile Site." In *Proceedings of the 7th International Ocean Disposal Symposium,* 625–43. Ottawa: Environment Canada.

APPENDIX: CASE STUDY EXAMPLES OF THE APPLICATION OF PROBABILISTIC RISK ANALYSIS IN U.S. ENVIRONMENTAL PROTECTION AGENCY REGULATORY DECISION MAKING

A. OVERVIEW

This Appendix focuses on examples of how probabilistic risk analysis (PRA) approaches have been used at EPA to inform regulatory decisions. The Appendix was prepared by representatives from various EPA program offices and regions currently involved in the development and application of PRA techniques. The Technical Panel selected the case study examples based on the members' knowledge of the specific PRA procedures, the types of techniques demonstrated, the availability to the reader through the Internet and the condition of having been peer reviewed; they also were selected to be illustrative of a spectrum of PRA used at EPA. The case studies are not designed to provide an exhaustive discussion of the wide variety of applications of PRA used within the Agency, but to highlight specific examples reflecting the range of approaches currently applied within EPA.

This Appendix is intended to serve as a resource for managers faced with decisions regarding when to apply PRA techniques to inform environmental decisions, and for exposure and risk assessors who may not be familiar with the wide variety of available PRA approaches. The document outlines categories of PRAs classified by the complexity of analysis to aid the decision-making process. This approach identifies various PRA tools, which include techniques ranging from a simple sensitivity analysis (e.g., identification of key exposure parameters or data visualization) requiring limited time, resources and expertise to develop (Group 1); to probabilistic approaches, including Monte Carlo analysis, that provide tools for evaluating variability and uncertainty separately and that require more resources and specialized expertise (Group 2); to sophisticated techniques of expert elicitation that generally require significant investment of employee time, additional expertise and external peer review (Group 3).

The case studies in this Appendix used PRA techniques within this ranked framework to provide additional information for managers. The case study summaries are provided in a format designed to highlight how the results of the PRAs were considered in decision making. These summaries include specific information on the conduct of the analyses as an aid in determining what tools might be appropriate to develop specific exposure or risk assessments for other sites.

The case studies range from examples of less resource-intensive analyses, which might assist in identifying key exposure parameters or the need for more data, to more detailed and resource-intensive approaches. Examples of applications in human health and ecological risk assessment include the exposure of children to chromated copper arsenate (CCA)-treated wood, the relation between particulates in air and health, dietary exposures to pesticides, modeling sea level change, sampling watersheds, and modeling bird and animal exposures.

B. INTRODUCTION

Historically, EPA has used deterministic risk assessments, or point estimates of risk, to evaluate cancer risks and noncancer health hazards to high-end exposed individuals (90th percentile or higher) and the average exposed individual (50th percentile) and, where appropriate, risks and hazards to populations, as required by specific environmental laws (USEPA 1992a). The use of default values for exposure parameters in risk assessments provides a procedural consistency that allows risk assessments to be feasible and tractable (USEPA 2004). The methods typically used in EPA deterministic risk assessments (DRA) rely on a combination of point values—some conservative and some typical—yielding a point estimate of exposure that is at some unknown point in the range of possible risks (USEPA 2004).

This Appendix presents case studies of PRA conducted by EPA over the past 10 to 15 years. Table A-1 summarizes the case studies by title, technique demonstrated, classification as a human health risk assessment (HHRA) or ecological risk assessment (ERA), and the program or regional office responsible for developing the case studies. This Appendix, provides a "snapshot" of the utilization of PRA across various programs in EPA.

C. OVERALL APPROACH TO PROBABILISTIC RISK ANALYSIS AT THE U.S. ENVIRONMENTAL PROTECTION AGENCY

C.1. U.S. Environmental Protection Agency Guidance and Policies on Probabilistic Risk Analysis

The case studies presented here build on the principles of PRA outlined in EPA's 1997 *Policy for Use of Probabilistic Analysis in Risk Assessment at the U.S. Environmental Protection Agency* (USEPA 1997a) and *Guiding Principles for Monte Carlo Analysis* (USEPA 1997b), as well as subsequent guidance documents on developing and using PRA. Guidance has been developed for the Agency and individual programs. Specific documents that refer to the use of PRA include the *Risk Assessment Guidance for Superfund: Volume III* (USEPA 2001); Risk Assessment Forum (RAF) *Framework for Ecological Risk Assessment* (USEPA 1992b); *Guidelines for Ecological Risk Assessment* (USEPA 1998); *Guidance for Risk Characterization* (USEPA 1995a); *Policy on Evaluating Health Risks to Children* (USEPA 1995b); *Policy for Use of Probabilistic Analysis in Risk Assessment* (USEPA 1997a); *Guidance on Cumulative Risk Assessment, Part 1: Planning and Scoping* (USEPA 1997c); and *Risk Characterization Handbook* (USEPA 2000a); and *Framework for Human Health Risk Assessment to Inform Decision Making* (USEPA 2014).

As shown in the individual case studies, the range and scope of the PRA will depend on the overall objectives of the decision that the analysis will inform. The *Guiding Principles for Monte Carlo Analysis* (USEPA 1997b) lay out the general approach that should be taken in all cases, beginning with defining the problem and scope of the assessment to selecting the best tools and approach. The *Guiding Principles* also describe the process of estimating and characterizing variability and uncertainty around risk estimates. Stahl and Cimorelli (2005) and the *Risk Assessment Guidance for Superfund: Volume III* (USEPA 2001) highlight the importance of communication between the risk assessor and manager. Stahl and Cimorelli (2005) and Jamieson (1996) indicate that it is important to determine whether a particular level of uncertainty is acceptable or not. The authors also suggest that this decision depends on context, values and regulatory policy. The *Risk Assessment Guidance for Superfund: Volume III* (Chapter 2 and Appendix F in USEPA 2001) describes a process for determining the appropriate level of PRA using a ranked approach from the less resource- and time-intensive approaches to more sophisticated analyses. Furthermore, the *Risk Assessment Guidance for Superfund: Volume III* outlines a process for developing a PRA work plan and a checklist for PRA reviewers (Chapter 2 and Appendix F in USEPA 2001). This guidance also provides information regarding how to communicate PRA results to decision makers and stakeholders (Chapter 6 in USEPA 2001).

C.2. Categorizing Case Studies

The ranked approach used for categorization is a process for a systematic, informed progression to increasingly complex risk assessment methods of PRA, which is outlined in the *Risk Assessment Guidance for Superfund* (USEPA 2001). The use of categories provides a framework for evaluating the various techniques of PRA. Higher categories reflect increasing complexity and often will require more time and resources. Higher categories also reflect increasing characterization of variability and uncertainty in the risk estimate, which may be important for making specific risk management decisions. Central to the approach is a systematic, informed progression using an iterative process of evaluation, deliberation, data collection, planning and scoping, development, and updates to the work plan and communication. All of these steps focus on deciding:

1. Whether or not the risk assessment, in its current state (e.g., DRA) is sufficient to support decisions (i.e., a clear path to exiting the process is available at each step).

2. If the assessment is determined to be insufficient, whether or not progression to a higher level of complexity (or refinement of the current analyses) would provide a sufficient benefit to warrant the additional effort of performing a PRA.

This Appendix groups case studies according to level of effort and complexity of the analysis and the increasing sophistication of the methods used (Table A-1). Although each group generally represents increasing effort and cost, this may not always be true. The groups also are intended to reflect the progression from simple to complex analysis that is determined by the interactive planning and scoping efforts of the risk assessors and managers. The use of particular terms to describe the groups, including "tiers," was avoided due to specific programmatic and regulatory connotations.

Group 1 Case Studies

Assessments within this group typically involve a sensitivity analysis and serve as an initial screening step in the risk assessment. Sensitivity analyses identify important parameters in the assessment where additional investigation may be helpful (Kurowicka and Cooke 2006). Sensitivity analysis can be simple or involve more complex mathematical and statistical techniques, such as correlation and regression analysis, to determine which factors in a risk model contribute most to the variance in the risk estimate.

Within the sensitivity analyses, a range of techniques is available: simple, "back-of-the-envelope" calculations, where the risk parameters are evaluated using a range of exposure parameters to determine the parameter that contributes most significantly to the risk (Case Study 1); analyses to rank the relative contributions of variables to the overall risk (Case Study 2); and data visualization using graphical techniques to array the data or Monte Carlo simulations (e.g., scatter plots).

More sophisticated analyses may include sensitivity ratios (e.g., elasticity); sensitivity scores (e.g., weighted sensitivity ratios); correlation coefficient or coefficient of determination; r^2 (e.g., Pearson product moment, Spearman rank); normalized multiple regression coefficients; and goodness-of-fit tests for subsets of the risk distribution (USEPA 2001).

The sensitivity analyses typically require minimal resources and time. Results of the sensitivity analyses are useful in identifying key parameters where additional Group 2 or Group 3 analyses may be appropriate. Sensitivity analyses also are helpful in identifying key parameters where additional research will have the highest impact on the risk assessment.

Group 2 Case Studies

Case studies within this group include a more sophisticated application of probabilistic tools, including PRA of specific exposure parameters (Case Studies 3 and 4), one-dimensional analyses (Case Study 5) and probabilistic sensitivity analysis (Case Studies 6 and 7).

The Group 2 case studies require larger time commitments for development, specialized expertise and additional analysis of exposure parameter data sources. Depending on the nature of the analysis, peer involvement or peer review may be appropriate to evaluate the products of the analysis.

Group 3 Case Studies

Assessments within this group are the most resource- and time-intensive analyses of the three categories. Risk analyses include two-dimensional Monte Carlo analysis (2-D MCA) that evaluates model variability and uncertainty (Case Studies 8, 9 and 10); microexposure event analysis (MEE), in which long-term exposure of an individual is simulated as the sum of separate short-term exposure events (Case Study 11); and probabilistic analysis (Case Studies 12 and 13).

Other types of analyses within this group include the expert elicitation method that is a systematic process of formalizing and quantifying, in terms of probabilities, experts' judgments about uncertain quantities (Case Studies 14 and 15); Bayesian statistics, which is a specialized branch of statistics that views the probability of an event occurring as the degree of belief or confidence in that occurrence (Case Study 16); and geostatistical analysis, which is another specialized branch of statistics that explicitly takes into account the geo-referenced context of the data and the information (e.g., attributes) attached to the data.

The Group 3 analyses require additional time and expertise in the planning and analysis of the assessment. Within this group, the level of expertise and resource commitments may vary with the techniques. Expert elicitation, for example, requires significantly more time for planning, identification of experts and meetings, when compared with the other techniques.

Table A-1. Case Study Examples of EPA Applications of Deterministic and Probabilistic Risk Assessment Techniques

Case Study Number	Title and Case Study Description	Type of Risk Assessment	Office/Region
Group 1: Point Estimate—Sensitivity Analysis			
1	**Sensitivity Analysis of Key Variables in Probabilistic Assessment of Children's Exposure to Arsenic in Chromated Copper Arsenate (CCA) Pressure-Treated Wood.** This case study demonstrates use of a point estimate sensitivity analysis to identify exposure variables critical to the analysis summarized in Case Study 9. The sensitivity analysis identified critical areas for future research and data collection and better characterized the amount of dislodgeable residue that exists on the wood surface.	Human Health	Office of Research and Development (ORD) and Office of Pesticide Programs (OPP)
2	**Assessment of the Relative Contribution of Atmospheric Deposition to Watershed Contamination.** An example of a workbook that demonstrates how "back-of-the-envelope" analysis of potential exposure rates can be used to target resources to identify other inputs before further analysis of air inputs in watershed contamination. Identification of key variables aided in identifying uncertainties and data gaps to target resource expenditures for further analysis. A case study example of the application of this technique also is identified.	Ecological	ORD
Group 2: Probabilistic Risk Analysis, One-Dimensional Monte Carlo Analysis (1-D MCA) and Probabilistic Sensitivity Analysis			
Group 2: Probabilistic Risk Analysis			
3	**Probabilistic Assessment of Angling Duration Used in the Assessment of Exposure to Hudson River Sediments via Consumption of Contaminated Fish.** A probabilistic analysis of one parameter in an exposure assessment—the time an individual fishes in a large river system. Development of site-specific information regarding exposure, with an existing data set for this geographic area, was needed to represent this exposed population. This information was used in the one-dimensional PRA described in Case Study 5.	Human Health	Superfund/ Region 2 (New York)
4	**Probabilistic Analysis of Dietary Exposure to Pesticides for Use in Setting Tolerance Levels.** The probabilistic Dietary Exposure Evaluation Model (DEEM) provides more accurate information on the range and probability of possible exposures.	Human Health	OPP

Table A-1. Case Study Examples of EPA Applications of Deterministic and Probabilistic Risk Assessment Techniques

Case Study Number	Title and Case Study Description	Type of Risk Assessment	Office/Region
Group 2: One-Dimensional Monte Carlo Analysis (1-D MCA)			
5	**One-Dimensional Probabilistic Risk Analysis of Exposures to Polychlorinated Biphenyls (PCBs) via Consumption of Fish From a Contaminated Sediment Site.** An example of a one-dimensional PRA (1-D MCA) of the *variability* of exposure as a function of the variability of individual exposure factors to evaluate the risks to anglers who consume recreationally caught fish from a PCB-contaminated river.	Human Health	Superfund/ Region 2 (New York)
Group 2: Probabilistic Sensitivity Analysis			
6	**Probabilistic Sensitivity Analysis of Knowledge Elicitation of the Concentration-Response Relationship Between PM$_{2.5}$ Exposure and Mortality.** An example of how the probabilistic analysis tools can be used to conduct a probabilistic sensitivity analysis following an expert elicitation (Group 3) presented in Case Study 14.	Human Health	Office of Air and Radiation (OAR)
7	**Environmental Monitoring and Assessment Program (EMAP): Using Probabilistic Sampling Techniques to Evaluate the Nation's Ecological Resources.** A probability-based sampling program designed to provide unbiased estimates of the condition of an aquatic resource over a large geographic area based on a small number of samples.	Ecological	ORD
Group 3: Advanced Probabilistic Risk Analysis—Two-Dimensional Monte Carlo Analysis (2-D MCA) Including Microexposure Modeling, Bayesian Statistics, Geostatistics and Expert Elicitation			
Group 3: Two-Dimensional Probabilistic Risk Analysis			
8	**Two-Dimensional Probabilistic Risk Analysis of *Cryptosporidium* in Public Water Supplies, With Bayesian Approaches to Uncertainty Analysis.** An analysis of the variability in the occurrence of *Cryptosporidium* in raw water supplies and in the treatment efficiency, as well as the uncertainty in these inputs. This case study includes an analysis of the dose-response relationship for *Cryptosporidium* infection.	Human Health	Office of Water (OW)
9	**Two-Dimensional Probabilistic Model of Children's Exposure to Arsenic in Chromated Copper Arsenate (CCA) Pressure-Treated Wood.** A two-dimensional model that addresses both variability and uncertainty in the exposures of children to CCA pressure-treated wood. The analysis was built on the sensitivity analysis described in Case Study 2.	Human Health	OPP/ORD

Table A-1. Case Study Examples of EPA Applications of Deterministic and Probabilistic Risk Assessment Techniques

Case Study Number	Title and Case Study Description	Type of Risk Assessment	Office/Region
10	**Two-Dimensional Probabilistic Exposure Assessment of Ozone.** A probabilistic exposure assessment that addresses short-term exposures to ozone. Population exposure to ambient ozone levels was evaluated using EPA's Air Pollutants Exposure (APEX) model, also referred to as the Total Risk Integrated Methodology/Exposure (TRIM.Expo) model.	Human Health	OAR
Group 3: Microexposure Event Analysis			
11	**Analysis of Microenvironmental Exposures to Fine Particulate Matter (PM$_{2.5}$) for a Population Living in Philadelphia, Pennsylvania.** A microexposure event analysis to simulate individual exposures to PM$_{2.5}$ in specific microenvironments, including the outdoors, indoor residences, offices, schools, stores and a vehicle.	Human Health	Region 3 (Philadelphia) and ORD
Group 3: Probabilistic Analysis			
12	**Probabilistic Analysis in Cumulative Risk Assessment of Organophosphorus Pesticides.** A probabilistic computer software program used to integrate various pathways, while simultaneously incorporating the time dimensions of the input data to calculate margins of exposure.	Human Health	OPP
13	**Probabilistic Ecological Effects Risk Assessment Models for Evaluating Pesticide Uses.** A multimedia exposure/ effects model that evaluates acute mortality levels in generic or specific avian species over a user-defined exposure window.	Ecological	OPP
Group 3: Expert Elicitation and Bayesian Belief Network			
14	**Expert Elicitation of Concentration-Response Relationship Between Fine Particulate Matter (PM$_{2.5}$) Exposure and Mortality.** A knowledge elicitation used to derive probabilistic estimates of the uncertainty in one element of a cost-benefit analysis used to support the PM$_{2.5}$ regulations.	Human Health	ORD/ OAR
15	**Expert Elicitation of Sea-Level Change Resulting From Global Climate Change.** An example of a PRA that describes the probability of sea level rise and parameters that predict sea level change.	Ecological	Office of Policy, Planning, and Evaluation

Table A-1. Case Study Examples of EPA Applications of Deterministic and Probabilistic Risk Assessment Techniques

Case Study Number	Title and Case Study Description	Type of Risk Assessment	Office/Region
16	**Knowledge Elicitation for Bayesian Belief Network Model of Stream Ecology.** An example of a Bayesian belief network model of the effect of increased fine-sediment load in a stream on macroinvertebrate populations.	Ecological	ORD

D. CASE STUDY SUMMARIES

D.1. Group 1 Case Studies

Case Study 1: Sensitivity Analysis of Key Variables in Probabilistic Assessment of Children's Exposure to Arsenic in Chromated Copper Arsenate Pressure-Treated Wood

This case study provides an example of the application of sensitivity analysis to identify important variables for population exposure variability for a Group 2 assessment (Case Study 9) and to indicate areas for further research. Specifically, EPA's Office of Research and Development (ORD), in collaboration with the Office of Pesticide Programs (OPP), used sensitivity analyses to identify the key variables in children's exposure to CCA-treated wood.

Approach. The sensitivity analyses used two approaches. The first approach estimated baseline exposure by running the exposure model with each input variable set to its median (50th percentile) value. Next, alternative exposure estimates were made by setting each input to its 25th or 75th percentile value while holding all other inputs at their median values. The ratio of the exposure estimate calculated when an input was estimated at its 25th or 75th percentile to the exposure estimate calculated when the input was at its median value provided a measure of that input's importance to the overall exposure assessment. The second approach applied a multiple stepwise regression analysis to the data points generated from the first approach. The correlation between the input variables and the exposure estimates provided an alternative measure of the input variable's relative importance in the exposure assessment. These two approaches were used in tandem to identify the critical inputs to the exposure assessment model.

Results of Analysis. The two sensitivity analyses together identified six critical input variables that most influenced the exposure assessment. The critical input variables were: wood surface residue-to-skin transfer efficiency, wood surface residue levels, fraction of hand surface area mouthed per mouthing event, average fraction of nonresidential outdoor time spent playing on a CCA-treated playset, frequency of hand washing and frequency of hand-to-mouth activity.

Management Considerations. The results of the sensitivity analyses were used to identify the most important input parameters in the treated wood risk assessments. The process also identified critical areas for future research. In particular, the assessment pointed to a need to collect data on the amount of dislodgeable residue that is transferred from the wood surface to a child's hand upon contact, and to better characterize the amount of dislodgeable residue that exists on the wood surface.

Selected References. The final report on the probabilistic exposure assessment of CCA-treated wood:

Zartarian, V. G., J. Xue, H. A. Özkaynak, W. Dang, G. Glen, L. Smith, and C. Stallings. *A Probabilistic Exposure Assessment for Children Who Contact CCA-Treated Playsets and Decks Using the Stochastic Human Exposure and Dose Simulation Model for the Wood Preservative Scenario (SHEDS-WOOD), Final Report.* EPA/600/X-05/009. Washington, D.C.: USEPA.

See also: Xue, J., V. G. Zartarian, H. Özkaynak, W. Dang, G. Glen, L. Smith, and C. Stallings. 2006. "A Probabilistic Exposure Assessment for Children Who Contact Chromated Copper Arsenate (CCA)-Treated Playsets and Decks, Part 2: Sensitivity and Uncertainty Analyses." *Risk Analysis* 26:533–41.

Case Study 2: Assessment of the Relative Contribution of Atmospheric Deposition to Watershed Contamination

Watershed contamination can result from several different sources, including the direct release of pollution into a water body, input from upstream water bodies and deposition from airborne sources. Efforts to control water body contamination begin with an analysis of the environmental sources to identify the parameters that provide the greatest contribution and determine where mitigation and/or analysis resources should be directed.

Approach. This case study provides an example of a "back-of-the-envelope" deterministic analysis of the contribution of air deposition to overall watershed nitrogen? Nutrient? contamination to identify uncertainties and/or data gaps, as well as to target resource expenditures. Nitrogen inputs have been studied in several east and Gulf Coast estuaries due to concerns about eutrophication. Nitrogen from atmospheric deposition is estimated to be as high as 10 to 40 percent of the total input of nitrogen to many of these estuaries, and perhaps higher in a few cases. For a watershed that has not been studied yet, a back-of-the-envelope calculation could be prepared based on information about the nitrogen deposition rates measured in a similar area. To estimate the deposition load directly to the water body, one would multiply the nitrogen deposition rate by the area of the water body. The analyst then could estimate the nitrogen load from other sources (e.g., point source discharges and runoff) to estimate a total nitrogen load for the water body. The estimate of loading due to atmospheric deposition then could be divided by the total nitrogen load for the water body to estimate the percent of contribution directly to the water body from atmospheric deposition.

The May 2003 report by the Casco Bay Air Deposition Study Team titled *Estimating Pollutant Loading From Atmospheric Deposition Using Casco Bay, Maine as a Case Study* is an analysis using the methodology described above. The Casco Bay Estuary, located in southwestern Maine, is used as a case study. The paper also includes the results of a field air deposition monitoring program conducted in Casco Bay from 1998 to 2000 and favorably compares the estimates developed for the rate of deposition of nitrogen, mercury and polycyclic aromatic hydrocarbons (PAHs) to the field monitoring results. The estimation approach is a useful starting point for understanding the sources of pollutants entering water bodies that cannot be accounted for through runoff or point source discharges.

Results of Analysis. The approach outlined above was applied to the Casco Bay Estuary in Maine. Resources, tools and strategies for pollution abatement can be effectively targeted at priority sources if estuaries are to be protected. Understanding the sources and annual loading of contaminants to an estuary facilitates good water quality management by defining the range of controls of both air and water pollution needed to achieve a desired result. The cost of conducting monitoring to determine atmospheric loading to a water body can be prohibitively high. Also, collection of monitoring data is a long-term undertaking because a minimum of 3 years of data is advisable to "smooth out" inter-annual variability. The estimation techniques described in this paper can serve as a useful and inexpensive "first-cut" at understanding the importance of the atmosphere as a pollution source and can help to identify areas where field measurements are needed to guide future management decisions.

Management Considerations. If a review of information on air deposition available for the analysis indicates a wide range of potential deposition rates, further study of this input would lead to better characterization of the air contribution to overall contamination. If the back-of-the envelope analysis suggests that air deposition is very small relative to other inputs, then resources should be targeted at studying or reducing other inputs before proceeding with further analysis of the air inputs.

Selected References. The back-of-the-envelope calculation is outlined in *Frequently Asked Questions about Atmospheric Deposition: A Handbook for Watershed Managers.* http://www.epa.gov/air/oaqps/gr8water/handbook/airdep_sept.pdf.

Further analysis is available in *Deposition of Air Pollutants to the Great Waters—Third Report to Congress.* http://www.epa.gov/air/oaqps/gr8water/3rdrpt/index.html.

The Casco Bay Estuary example is available at http://epa.gov/owow/airdeposition/cascobay.pdf.

D.2. Group 2 Case Studies

Case Study 3: Probabilistic Assessment of Angling Duration Used in the Assessment of Exposure to Hudson River Sediments via Consumption of Contaminated Fish

In assessing the health impact of contaminated Superfund sites, exposure duration typically is assumed to be the same as the length of time that an individual lives in a specific area (i.e., residence duration). In conducting the HHRA for the Hudson River Polychlorinated Biphenyl (PCB) Superfund Site, however, there was concern that exposure duration based on residence duration may underestimate the time spent fishing (i.e., angling duration).

Risk Analysis. An individual may move from one residence to another and continue to fish in the same location, or an individual may choose to stop fishing irrespective of the location of his or her home. EPA Region 2 developed a site-specific distribution of angling duration using the fishing patterns reported in a New York State-wide angling survey (Connelly *et al.* 1990) and migration data for the five counties surrounding more than 40 miles of the Upper Hudson River collected as part of the U.S. Census.

Results of Analysis. The 50th and 95th percentile values from the distribution of angling durations were higher than the default values based on residence duration using standard default exposure assumptions for residential scenarios. These values were used as a base for the central tendency and reasonable maximum exposure point estimates, respectively, in the deterministic assessment.

Management Considerations. The information provided in this analysis was used in the point estimate analysis. The full distribution was used in conducting a Group 2 PRA for the fish consumption pathway, which is presented as Case Study 5.

Selected References. The final risk assessment was released in November 2000 and is available at http://www.epa.gov/hudson/reports.htm.

Further information, including EPA's January 2002 response to comments on the risk assessment, is available at http://www.epa.gov/hudson/ResponsivenessSummary.pdf.

Case Study 4: Probabilistic Analysis of Dietary Exposure to Pesticides for Use in Setting Tolerance Levels

Under the Federal Food, Drug, and Cosmetic Act (FFDCA), EPA may authorize a tolerance or exemption from the requirement of a tolerance to allow a pesticide residue in food, only if the Agency determines that such residues would be "safe." This determination is made by estimating exposure to the pesticide and comparing the estimated exposure to a toxicological benchmark dose. Until 1998, the OPP used a software program called the Dietary Risk Evaluation System (DRES) to conduct its acute dietary risk assessments for pesticide residues in foods. Acute assessments conducted with DRES assumed that 100 percent of a given crop with registered use of a pesticide was treated with that pesticide and all such treated crop items contained pesticide residues at the maximum legal (tolerance) level, matching this to a reasonably high consumption value (around the 95th percentile). The resulting DRES acute risk estimates were considered "high-end" or "bounding" estimates. It was not possible, however, to know where the pesticide exposure estimates from the DRES software fit in the overall distribution of exposures due to the limits of the tools being used.

To address these deficiencies, OPP developed an acute probabilistic dietary exposure guidance to use a model that would estimate the exposure to pesticides in the food supply. Rather than the crude "high-end," single-point estimates provided by deterministic assessments, the probabilistic Dietary Exposure Evaluation Model (DEEM) provides specific information about the range and probability of possible exposures. Depending on the characterization of the input, this could include the 95th percentile regulation—generally for lower tiers that do not include the percent of crop treated—to the 99.9th percentile for the more refined assessments, which would include the percent of crop treated information.

Probabilistic Analysis. This case study provides an example of a one-dimensional PRA of dietary exposure to pesticides (Group 2). The DEEM generates acute, probabilistic dietary exposure assessments using data on: (1) the distribution of daily consumption of specific commodities (e.g., wheat, corn and apples) by specific individuals; and (2) the distribution of concentrations of a specific pesticide in those food commodities. Data on commodity consumption are collected by the U.S. Department of Agriculture (USDA) in its Continuing Survey of Food Intake by Individuals (CSFII). Pesticide residue concentrations on food commodities are generally obtained from crop field trials, USDA's Pesticide Data Program (PDP), U.S. Food and Drug Administration (FDA) monitoring data, or market basket surveys. Using these data, DEEM is able to calculate an estimate of the risk to the general U.S. population, in addition to 26 population subgroups, including 5 subgroups for infants and children (infants less than 1, children 1 to 2, children 3 to 5, youths 6 to 12 and teens 13 to 19 years of age).

Results of Analysis. DEEM has been used in risk assessments to support tolerance levels for several pesticides (e.g., phosalone) and as part of cumulative risk assessments for organophosphorus compounds (see Case Study 12) and other pesticides.

Management Considerations. Using the DRES, decisions were being made without a complete representation of the distribution of risk among the population and without full knowledge of where in the distribution of risk the DRES risk estimate lay. This was of concern not only for regulators interested in public health protection, but also for the pesticide registrants who could argue that the Agency was arbitrarily selecting the level at which to regulate. For most cases reviewed by OPP to date, estimated exposure at the 99.9th percentile calculated by DEEM probabilistic techniques is significantly lower than exposure calculated using DRES-type deterministic assumptions at the unknown percentile.

Selected References. A link to the DEEM model is available at http://www.epa.gov/pesticides/science/deem/index.html.

Case Study 5: One-Dimensional Probabilistic Risk Analysis of Exposure to Polychlorinated Biphenyls via Consumption of Fish From a Contaminated Sediment Site

EPA Region 2 conducted a preliminary deterministic HHRA at the Hudson River PCBs Superfund site. The DRA demonstrated that consumption of recreationally caught fish provided the highest exposure among relevant exposure pathways, which resulted in cancer risks and noncancer health hazards that exceeded regulatory benchmarks.

Probabilistic Analysis. Because of the size, complexity and high level of public interest in this site, EPA Region 2 implemented a Group 2 probabilistic assessment to characterize the variability in risks associated with the fish consumption exposure pathway. The analysis was a one-dimensional Monte Carlo analysis (1-D MCA) of the *variability* of exposure as a function of the variability of individual exposure factors. Uncertainty was assessed using sensitivity analysis of the input variables. Data to characterize the distributions of exposure parameters were drawn from the published literature (e.g., fish consumption rate) or from existing databases, such as the U.S. Census data (e.g., angling duration, see Case Study 3). Mathematical models of the environmental fate, transport and bioaccumulation of PCBs in the Hudson River previously developed were used to forecast changes in PCB concentration over time.

Results of Analysis. The results of the PRA were consistent with the deterministic results. For the central tendency individual, point estimates were near the median (50th percentile). For the reasonable maximum exposure (RME) individual, point estimate values were at or above the 95th percentile of the probabilistic analysis. The DRA and PRA were the subject of a formal peer review by a panel of independent experts.

The Monte Carlo-based case scenario is the one from which point estimate exposure factors for fish ingestion were drawn; thus, the point estimate RMEs and the Monte Carlo-based case estimates can be compared. Similarly, the point estimate central tendency (average) and the Monte Carlo-based case midpoint (50th percentile) are comparable. For cancer risk, the point estimate RME for fish ingestion (1×10^{-3}) falls approximately at the 95th percentile from the Monte Carlo-based case analysis. The point estimate central tendency value (3×10^{-5}) and the Monte Carlo-based case 50th percentile value (6×10^{-5}) are similar. For noncancer health hazards, the point estimate RME for fish ingestion (104 for a young child 1 to 6 years of age) falls between the 95th and 99th percentiles of the Monte Carlo-based case. The point estimate central tendency hazard index (HI; 12 for a young child) is approximately equal to the 50th percentile of the Monte Carlo-based case HI of 11.

Figures A-1 and A-2 provide a comparison of results from the probabilistic analysis with that of the DRA for cancer risks and noncancer health hazards. Figures A-1 and A-2 plot percentiles for 72 combinations of exposure variables (e.g., distributions from creel angler surveys' residence duration, fishing locations and cooking losses) of the noncancer HI values and the cancer risks, respectively. In each of these figures, the variability of cancer risk or noncancer HIs for anglers within the exposed population is plotted on the y-axis for particular percentiles within the population. This variability is a function of the variations in fish consumption rates, fishing duration, differences in fish species ingested and so forth. The uncertainty in the estimates is indicated by the range of either cancer risk or noncancer HI values plotted on the x-axis. This uncertainty is a function of the 72 combinations of the exposure factor inputs examined in the sensitivity analysis. This analysis provides a semi-quantitative confidence interval for the cancer risks and HI values at any particulate percentile. As these figures show, the intervals span somewhat less than two orders of magnitude (e.g., < 100-fold). The vertical lines indicate the deterministic endpoints.

Management Considerations. Early and continued involvement of the community improved public acceptance of the results. In addition, careful consideration of the methods used to present the probabilistic results to the public lead to greater understanding of the findings.

Selected References. The final risk assessment was released in November 2000 and is available at http://www.epa.gov/hudson/reports.htm.

Further information, including EPA's January 2002 response to comments on the risk assessment, is available at http://www.epa.gov/hudson/ResponsivenessSummary.pdf.

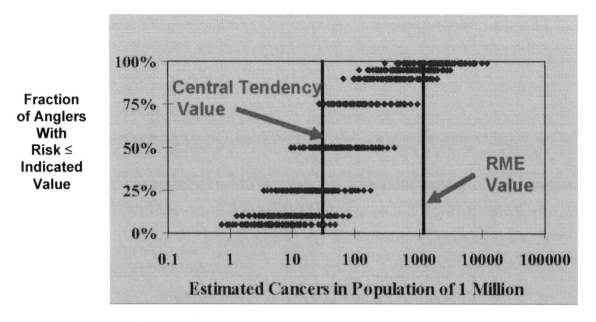

Figure A-1. Monte Carlo Cancer Summary Based on a One-Dimensional Probabilistic Risk Analysis of Exposure to Polychlorinated Biphenyls. The estimated cancer rate was calculated based on the consumption of fish from a contaminated sediment site. Source: USEPA 2000b.

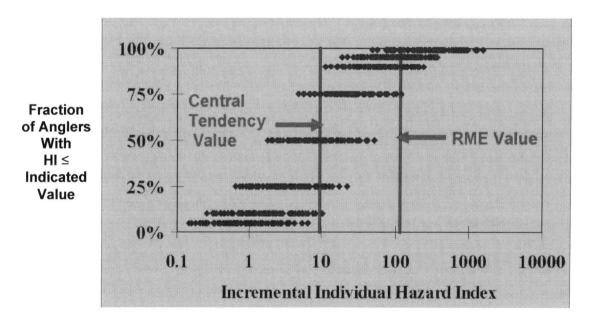

Figure A-2. Monte Carlo Noncancer Hazard Index Summary Based on a One-Dimensional Probabilistic Risk Analysis of Exposure to Polychlorinated Biphenyls. The incremental individual hazard index (HI) was calculated based on the consumption of fish from a contaminated sediment site. Source: USEPA 2000b.

Case Study 6: Probabilistic Sensitivity Analysis of Expert Elicitation of Concentration-Response Relationship Between Fine Particulate Matter Exposure and Mortality

In 2002, the National Research Council (NRC) recommended that EPA improve its characterization of uncertainty in the benefits assessment for proposed regulations of air pollutants. NRC recommended that probability distributions for key sources of uncertainty be developed using available empirical data or through formal elicitation of expert judgments. In response to this recommendation, EPA conducted an expert elicitation evaluation of the concentration-response relationship between fine particulate matter ($PM_{2.5}$) exposure and mortality, a key component of the benefits assessment of the $PM_{2.5}$ regulation. Further information on the expert elicitation procedure and results is provided in Case Study 14. To evaluate the degree to which the results of the assessment depended on the judgments of individual experts or on the methods of expert elicitation, a probabilistic sensitivity analysis was performed on the results.

Probabilistic Analysis. The expert elicitation procedure used carefully constructed interviews to elicit from each of 12 experts an estimate of the probabilistic distribution for the average expected decrease in U.S. annual, adult, all-cause mortality associated with a 1 microgram per cubic meter ($\mu g/m^3$) decrease in annual average $PM_{2.5}$ levels. This case study provides an example of the use of probabilistic sensitivity analysis (Group 2) as one element of the overall assessment. For the sensitivity analysis, a simplified health benefits analysis was conducted to assess the sensitivity of the results to the responses of individual experts and to three factors in the study design: (1) the use of parametric or nonparametric approaches by experts to characterize their uncertainty in the $PM_{2.5}$ mortality coefficient; (2) participation in the Pre-Elicitation Workshop; and (3) allowing experts to change their judgments after the Post-Elicitation Workshop. The individual quantitative expert judgments were used to estimate a distribution of benefits, in the form of the number of deaths avoided, associated with a reduction in ambient, annual average $PM_{2.5}$ concentrations from 12 to 11 $\mu g/m^3$. The 12 individual distributions of estimated avoided deaths were pooled using equal weights to create a single overall distribution reflecting input from each expert. This distribution served as the baseline for the sensitivity analysis, which compared the means and standard deviations of the baseline distribution with several variants.

Results of Analysis. The first analysis examined the sensitivity of the mean and standard deviation of the overall mortality distribution to the removal of individual experts' distributions. In general, the results suggested a fairly equal division between those experts whose removal shifted the distribution mean up and those who shifted it down. There were relatively modest impacts of individual experts. The standard deviation of the combined distribution also was not affected strongly by the removal of individual experts. The second analysis evaluated whether the use of parametric or nonparametric approaches affected the overall results. The results suggested that the use of parametric distributions led to distributions with similar or slightly increased uncertainty compared with distributions provided by experts who offered percentiles of a nonparametric distribution. The last analysis evaluated whether participation in the Pre- or Post-Elicitation Workshops affected the results. Participation in either workshop did not appear to have a significant effect on experts' judgments based on measures of change in the baseline distribution. Overall, the sensitivity analyses demonstrated that the assessment was robust, with little dependence on individual experts' judgments or on the specific elicitation methods evaluated.

Management Considerations. The sensitivity analysis demonstrated the robustness of the $PM_{2.5}$ expert elicitation-based assessment by showing that the panel of experts was generally well balanced and that alternative elicitation methods would not have markedly altered the overall results.

Selected References. The details of this analysis are provided in the Industrial Economics, Inc., document titled: *Expanded Expert Judgment Assessment of the Concentration-Response Relationship Between PM$_{2.5}$ Exposure and Mortality,* Final Report, September 21, 2006. This document is available at http://www.epa.gov/ttn/ecas/regdata/Uncertainty/pm_ee_report.pdf.

The expert elicitation assessment, along with the Regulatory Impact Analysis (RIA) of the PM$_{2.5}$ standard, is available at http://www.epa.gov/ttn/ecas/ria.html.

Case Study 7: Environmental Monitoring and Assessment Program: Using Probabilistic Sampling to Evaluate the Condition of the Nation's Aquatic Resources

Monitoring is a key tool used to identify the locations where the environment is in a healthy biological condition and requires protection, and where environmental problems are occurring and need remediation. Most monitoring, however, is not performed in a way that allows for statistically valid assessments of water quality conditions in unmonitored waters (USGAO 2000). States thus cannot adequately measure the status and trends in water quality as required by the Clean Water Act (CWA) Section 305(b).

The Environmental Monitoring and Assessment Program's (EMAP) focus has been to develop unbiased statistical survey design frameworks and sensitive indicators that allow the condition of aquatic ecosystems to be assessed at state, regional and national scales. A cornerstone of EMAP has been the use of probabilistic sampling to allow representative, unbiased, cost-effective condition assessments for aquatic resources covering large areas. EMAP's statistical survey methods are very efficient, requiring relatively few sample locations to make valid scientific statements about the condition of aquatic resources over large areas (e.g., the condition of all of the wadeable streams in the western United States).

Probabilistic Analysis. This research program provides multiple case studies using probabilistic sampling designs for different aquatic resources (estuaries, streams and rivers). An EMAP probability-based sampling program delivers an unbiased estimate of the condition of an aquatic resource over a large geographic area from a small number of samples. The principal characteristics of a probabilistic sampling design are: the population being sampled is unambiguously described; every element in the population has the opportunity to be sampled with a known probability; and sample selection is conducted by a random process. This approach allows statistical confidence levels to be placed on the estimates and provides the potential to detect statistically significant changes and trends in condition with repeated sampling. In addition, this approach permits the aggregation of data collected from smaller areas to predict the condition of a large geographic area.

The EMAP design framework allows the selection of unbiased, representative sampling sites and specifies the information to be collected at these sites. The validity of the overall inference rests on the design and subsequent analysis to produce regionally representative information. The EMAP uses the approach outlined in the EPA's *Generalized Random Tessellation Stratified Spatially-Balanced Survey Designs for Aquatic Resources* (Olsen 2012). The spatially balanced aspect spreads out the sampling locations geographically, but still ensures that each element has an equal chance of being selected.

Results of Analysis. Data collected using the EMAP approach has allowed the Agency to make scientifically defensible assessments of the ecological condition of large geographic areas for reporting to Congress under CWA 305(b). The EMAP approach has been used to provide the first reports on the condition of the nation's estuaries, streams, rivers and lakes, and it is scheduled to be used for wetlands. EMAP findings have been included in EPA's Report on the Environment and the Heinz Center's The State of the Nation's Ecosystems. Data collected through an EMAP approach improve the ability to assess ecological progress in environmental protection and restoration, and provide valuable information for decision makers and the public. The use of probabilistic analysis methods allows meaningful assessment and regional comparisons of aquatic ecosystem conditions across the United States. Finally, the probabilistic approach provides scientific credibility for the monitoring network and aids in identifying data gaps.

Management Considerations. Use of an EMAP approach addresses criticisms from the Government Accountability Office (GAO), the National Academy of Sciences (NAS), the Heinz Center (a nonprofit environmental policy institution), and others that noted the nation lacked the data to make scientifically valid characterizations of water quality regionally and across the United States. The program provides cost-effective, scientifically defensible and representative data, to permit the evaluation of quantifiable trends in ecosystem condition, to support performance-based management and facilitate better public decisions regarding ecosystem management. EMAP's approach now has been adopted by EPA's Office of Water (OW) to collect data on the condition of all the nation's aquatic resources. OW, Office of Air and Radiation (OAR) and Office of Chemical Safety and Pollution Prevention (OCSPP; formerly the Office of Prevention, Pesticides, and Toxic Substances) now have environmental accountability endpoints using EMAP approaches in their Agency performance goals.

Selected References. General information concerning EMAP is available at http://www.epa.gov/emap/index.html.

Information on EMAP monitoring designs is available at http://www.epa.gov/nheerl/arm/designpages/monitdesign/monitoring_design_info.htm.

EPA's *Generalized Random Tessellation Stratified Spatially-Balanced Survey Designs for Aquatic Resources* document is available at http://www.epa.gov/nheerl/arm/documents/presents/grts_ss.pdf.

USGAO (U.S. Government Accountability Office). 2000. *Water Quality: Key EPA and State Decisions Limited by Inconsistent and Incomplete Data.* GAO/RCED-00-54. Washington, D.C.: USGAO. http://www.environmental-auditing.org/Portals/0/AuditFiles/useng00ar_ft_key_epa.pdf.

USEPA (U.S. Environmental Protection Agency). 2002. *EMAP Research Strategy.* Research Triangle Park, NC: Environmental Monitoring and Assessment Program, National Health and Environmental Effects Research Laboratory (NHEERL), USEPA. http://www.epa.gov/nheerl/emap/files/emap_research_strategy.pdf.

D.3. Group 3 Case Studies

Case Study 8: Two-Dimensional Probabilistic Risk Analysis of *Cryptosporidium* in Public Water Supplies, With Bayesian Approaches to Uncertainty Analysis

Probabilistic assessment of the occurrence and health effects associated with *Cryptosporidium* bacteria in public drinking water supplies was used to support the economic analysis of the final Long-Term 2 Enhanced Surface Water Treatment Rule (LT2). EPA's Office of Ground Water and Drinking Water (OGWDW) conducted this analysis and established a baseline disease burden attributable to *Cryptosporidium* in public water supplies that use surface water sources. Next, it modeled source water monitoring and finished water improvements that will be realized as a result of the LT2. Post-Rule risk is estimated and the LT2's health benefit is the result of subtracting this from the baseline disease burden.

Probabilistic Analysis. Probabilistic assessment was used for this analysis as a means of addressing the variability in the occurrence of *Cryptosporidium* in raw water supplies, the variability in the treatment efficiency, and the uncertainty in these inputs and in the dose-response relationship for *Cryptosporidium* infection. This case study provides an example of a PRA that evaluates both variability and uncertainty at the same time and is referred to as a two-dimensional PRA. The analysis also included probabilistic treatments of uncertain dose-response and occurrence parameters. Markov Chain Monte Carlo samples of parameter sets filled this function. This Bayesian approach (treating the unknown parameters as random variables) differs from classical treatments, which would regard the parameters as unknown, but fixed (Group 3: Advanced PRA). The risk analysis used existing datasets (e.g., the occurrence of *Cryptosporidium* and treatment efficacy) to inform the variability of these inputs. Uncertainty distributions were characterized based on professional judgment or by analyzing data using Bayesian statistical techniques.

Results of Analysis. The risk analysis identified the *Cryptosporidium* dose-response relationship as the most critical model parameters in the assessment, followed by the occurrence of the pathogen and treatment efficiency. By simulating implementation of the Rule using imprecise, biased measurement methods, the assessment provided estimates of the number of public water supply systems that would require corrective action and the nature of the actions likely to be implemented. This information afforded a realistic measure of the benefits (in reduced disease burden) expected with the LT2. In response to Science Advisory Board (SAB) comments, additional *Cryptosporidium* dose-response models were added to more fully reflect uncertainty in this element of the assessment.

Management Considerations. The LT2 underwent external peer review, review by EPA's SAB and intense review by the Office of Management and Budget (OMB). Occurrence and dose-response components of the risk analysis model were communicated to stakeholders during the Rule's Federal Advisory Committee Act (FACA) process. Due to the rigor of the analysis and the signed FACA "Agreement in Principle," the OMB review was straightforward.

Selected References. The final assessment of occurrence and exposure to *Cryptosporidium* was released in December 2005 and is available at
http://www.epa.gov/safewater/disinfection/lt2/regulations.html.

Case Study 9: Two-Dimensional Probabilistic Model of Children's Exposure to Arsenic in Chromated Copper Arsenate Pressure-Treated Wood

Probabilistic models were developed in response to EPA's October 2001 Federal Insecticide, Fungicide, and Rodenticide Act (FIFRA) Scientific Advisory Panel (SAP) recommendations to use probabilistic modeling to estimate children's exposures to arsenic in CCA-treated playsets and home decks.

Probabilistic Analysis. EPA's ORD, in collaboration with the Office of Pesticide Programs (OPP), developed and applied a probabilistic exposure assessment of children's exposure to arsenic and chromium from contact with CCA-treated wood playsets and decks. This case study provides an example of the use of two-dimensional (i.e., addressing both variability and uncertainty) probabilistic exposure assessment (Group 3: Advanced PRA). The two-dimensional assessment employed a modification of ORD's Stochastic Human Exposure and Dose Simulation (SHEDS) model to simulate children's exposure to arsenic and chromium from CCA-treated wood playsets and decks, as well as the surrounding soil. Staff from both ORD and OPP collaborated in the development of the SHEDS-Wood model.

Results of Analysis. A draft of the probabilistic exposure assessment received SAP review in December 2003; the final report was released in 2005. The results of the probabilistic exposure assessment were consistent with or in the range of the results of deterministic exposure assessments conducted by several other organizations. The model results were used to compare exposures under a variety of scenarios, including cold versus warm weather activity patterns, use of wood sealants to reduce the availability of contaminants on the surface of the wood, and different hand-washing frequencies. The modeling of alternative mitigation scenarios indicated that the use of sealants could result in the greatest exposure reduction, while increased frequency of hand washing also could reduce exposure.

OPP used the SHEDS-Wood model exposure results in its probabilistic children's risk assessment for CCA (USEPA 2008). This included recommendations for risk reduction (use of sealants and careful attention to children's hand washing) to homeowners with existing CCA wood structures. In addition, the exposure assessment was used to identify areas for further research, including: the efficacy of wood sealants in reducing dislodgeable contaminant residues, the frequency with which children play on or around CCA wood, and transfer efficiency and residue concentrations. To better characterize the efficacy of sealants in reducing exposure, EPA and the Consumer Product Safety Commission (CPSC) conducted a 2-year study of how dislodgeable contaminant residue levels changed with the use of various types of commercially available wood sealants.

Management Considerations. The OPP used SHEDS results directly in its final risk assessment for children playing on CCA-treated playground equipment and decks. The model enhanced risk assessment and management decisions and prioritized data needs related to wood preservatives. The modeling product was pivotal in the risk management and re-registration eligibility decisions for CCA, and in advising the public how to minimize health risks from existing treated wood structures. Industry also is using SHEDS to estimate exposures to CCA and other wood preservatives. Some states are using the risk assessment as guidance in setting their regulations for CCA-related playground equipment.

Selected References. The final probabilistic risk assessment based on the SHEDS-Wood exposure assessment is available at http://www.epa.gov/oppad001/reregistration/cca/final_cca_factsheet.htm.

The model results were included in the final report on the probabilistic exposure assessment of CCA-treated wood surfaces: Zartarian, V.G., J. Xue, H. A. Özkaynak, W. Dang, G. Glen, L. Smith, and C. Stallings. 2006. *A Probabilistic Exposure Assessment for Children Who Contact CCA-Treated Playsets and Decks Using the Stochastic Human Exposure and Dose Simulation Model for the Wood Preservative Scenario (SHEDS-Wood), Final Report.* EPA/600/X-05/009. Washington, D.C.: USEPA.

Results of the sealant studies were released in January 2007 and are available at http://www.epa.gov/oppad001/reregistration/cca/index.htm#reviews.

The results of the analysis were published as: Zartarian, V.G., J. Xue, H. Özkaynak, W. Dang, G. Glen, L. Smith, and C. Stallings. 2006. "A Probabilistic Arsenic Exposure Assessment for Children who Contact CAA-Treated Playsets and Decks, Part 1: Model Methodology, Variability Results, and Model Evaluation." *Risk Analysis* 26: 515–31.

More information on the analysis can be found by consulting the following resource:

USEPA (U.S. Environmental Protection Agency). 2008. *Case Study Examples of the Application of Probabilistic Risk Analysis in U.S. Environmental Protection Agency Regulatory Decision-Making (In Review).* Washington, D.C.: Risk Assessment Forum, USEPA

Case Study 10: Two-Dimensional Probabilistic Exposure Assessment of Ozone

As part of EPA's recent review of the ozone National Ambient Air Quality Standards (NAAQS), the Office of Air Quality Planning and Standards (OAQPS) conducted detailed probabilistic exposure and risk assessments to evaluate potential alternative standards for ozone. At different stages of this review, the Clean Air Scientific Advisory Committee (CASAC) Ozone Panel (an independent scientific review committee of EPA's SAB) and the public reviewed and provided comments on analyses and documents prepared by EPA. A scope and methods plan for the exposure and risk assessments was developed in 2005 (USEPA 2005). This plan was intended to facilitate consultation with the CASAC, as well as public review, and to obtain advice on the overall scope, approaches and key issues in advance of the completion of the analyses. This case study describes the probabilistic exposure assessment, which addresses short-term exposures to ozone. The exposure estimates were used as an input to the HHRA for lung function decrements in all children and asthmatic school-aged children based on exposure-response relationships derived from controlled human exposure studies.

Probabilistic Analysis. Population exposure to ambient ozone levels was evaluated using EPA's Air Pollutants Exposure (APEX) model, also referred to as the Total Risk Integrated Methodology/Exposure (TRIM.Expo) model. Exposure estimates were developed for recent ozone levels, based on 2002 to 2004 air quality data, and for ozone levels simulated to just meet the existing 0.08 ppm, 8-hour ozone NAAQS and several alternative ozone standards, based on adjusting the 2002 to 2004 air quality data. Exposure estimates were modeled for 12 urban areas located throughout the United States for the general population, all school-age children and asthmatic school-age children. This exposure assessment is described in a technical report (USEPA 2007b). The exposure model APEX is documented in a user's guide and technical document (USEPA 2006). A Monte Carlo approach was used to produce quantitative estimates of the uncertainty in the APEX model results, based on estimates of the uncertainties for the most important model inputs. The quantification of model input uncertainties, a discussion of model structure uncertainties, and the results of the uncertainty analysis are documented in Langstaff (2007).

Results of Analysis. Uncertainty in the APEX model predictions results from uncertainties in the spatial interpolation of measured concentrations, the microenvironment models and parameters, people's activity patterns, and to a lesser extent, model structure. The predominant sources of uncertainty appear to be the human activity pattern information and the spatial interpolation of ambient concentrations from monitoring sites to other locations. The primary policy-relevant finding was that the uncertainty in the exposure assessment is small enough to lend confidence to the use of the model results for the purpose of informing the Administrator's decision on the ozone standard.

Figure A-3 illustrates the uncertainty distribution for one model result, the percent of children with exposures above 0.08 ppm, 8-hour while at moderate exertion. The point estimate of 20 percent is the result from the APEX simulation using the best estimates of the model inputs. The corresponding result from the Monte Carlo simulations ranges from 17 to 26 percent, with a 95 percent uncertainty interval (UI) of 19 to 24 percent. Note that the UIs are not symmetric because the distributions are skewed.

Management Considerations. The exposure analysis also provided information on the frequency with which population exposures exceeded several potential health effect benchmark levels that were identified based on the evaluation of health effects in clinical studies.

The exposure and risk assessments are summarized in Chapters 4 and 5, respectively, of the *Ozone Staff Paper* (USEPA 2007a). The exposure estimates over these potential health effect benchmarks were part of the basis for the Administrator's March 27, 2008, decision to revise the ozone NAAQS from 0.08 to 0.075 ppm, 8-hour average (see the final rule for the ozone NAAQS[1]).

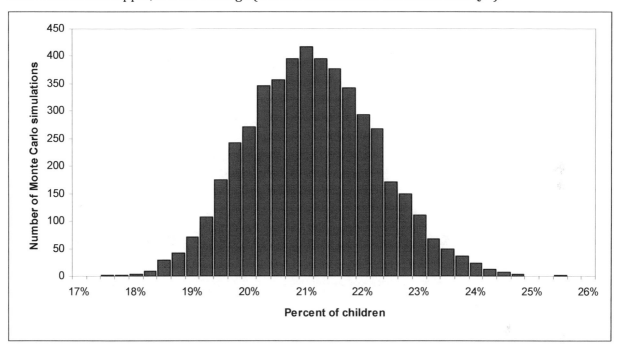

Figure A-3. Uncertainty Distribution Model Results. The estimated percentage of children with 8-hour exposures above 0.08 ppm at moderate exertion (the point estimate is 20%).

Selected References. More information on the analysis can be found by consulting the following resources:

Langstaff, J. E. 2007. *Analysis of Uncertainty in Ozone Population Exposure Modeling.* Office of Air Quality Planning and Standards Staff Memorandum to Ozone NAAQS Review Docket. OAR-2005-0172. http://www.epa.gov/ttn/naaqs/standards/ozone/s_ozone_cr_td.html

USEPA (U.S. Environmental Protection Agency). 2005. *Ozone Health Assessment Plan: Scope and Methods for Exposure Analysis and Risk Assessment.* Research Triangle Park, NC: Office of Air Quality Planning and Standards, USEPA. http://www.epa.gov/ttn/naaqs/standards/ozone/s_o3_cr_pd.html

USEPA. 2006. *Total Risk Integrated Methodology (TRIM)—Air Pollutants Exposure Model Documentation (TRIM.Expo/APEX, Version 4) Volume I: User's Guide; Volume II: Technical Support Document.* Research Triangle Park, NC: Office of Air Quality Planning and Standards, USEPA. June 2006. http://www.epa.gov/ttn/fera/human_apex.html

USEPA. 2007a. *Review of National Ambient Air Quality Standards for Ozone: Policy Assessment of Scientific and Technical Information—OAQPS Staff Paper.* Research Triangle Park, NC: Office of Air Quality Planning and Standards, USEPA. http://www.epa.gov/ttn/naaqs/standards/ozone/s_ozone_cr_sp.html

---

[1] National Ambient Air Quality Standards for Ozone, Final Rule. 73 Fed. Reg. 16436 (Mar. 27, 2008).

USEPA. 2007b. *Ozone Population Exposure Analysis for Selected Urban Areas.* Research Triangle Park, NC: Office of Air Quality Planning and Standards, USEPA.
http://www.epa.gov/ttn/naaqs/standards/ozone/s_ozone_cr_td.html

Case Study 11: Analysis of Microenvironmental Exposures to Fine Particulate Matter for a Population Living in Philadelphia, Pennsylvania

This case study used the Stochastic Human Exposure and Dose Simulation model for Particulate Matter (SHEDS-PM) developed by EPA's National Exposure Research Laboratory (NERL) to prepare a probabilistic assessment of population exposure to $PM_{2.5}$ in Philadelphia, Pennsylvania. This case study simulation was prepared to accomplish three goals: (1) estimate the contribution of $PM_{2.5}$ of ambient (outdoor) origin to total $PM_{2.5}$ exposure; (2) determine the major factors that influence personal exposure to $PM_{2.5}$; and (3) identify factors that contribute the greatest uncertainty to model predictions.

Probabilistic Analysis. The two-dimensional probabilistic assessment used a microexposure event technique to simulate individual exposures to $PM_{2.5}$ in specific microenvironments (outdoors, indoor residence, office, school, store, restaurant or bar, and in a vehicle). The population for the simulation was generated using demographic data at the census-tract level from the U.S. Census. Characteristics of the simulated individuals were selected randomly to match the demographic proportions within the census tract for gender, age, employment status and housing type. The assessment used spatially and temporally interpolated ambient $PM_{2.5}$ measurements from 1992 to 1993 and 1990 U.S. Census data for each census tract in Philadelphia. This case study provides an example of both two-dimensional (variability and uncertainty) probabilistic assessment and microexposure event assessment (Group 3: Advanced PRA).

Results of Analysis. Results of the analysis showed that human activity patterns did not have as strong an influence on ambient $PM_{2.5}$ exposures as was observed for exposure to indoor $PM_{2.5}$ sources. Exposure to $PM_{2.5}$ of ambient origin contributed a significant percent of the daily total $PM_{2.5}$ exposures, especially for the segment of the population without exposure to environmental tobacco smoke in the residence. Development of the SHEDS-PM model using the Philadelphia $PM_{2.5}$ case study also provided useful insights into data needs for improving inputs into the SHEDS-PM model, reducing uncertainty and further refinement of the model structure. Some of the important data needs identified from the application of the model include: daily $PM_{2.5}$ measurements over multiple seasons and across multiple sites within an urban area, improved capability of dispersion models to predict ambient $PM_{2.5}$ concentrations at greater spatial resolution and over a 1-year time period, measurement studies to better characterize the physical factors governing infiltration of ambient $PM_{2.5}$ into residential microenvironments, further information on particle-generating sources within the residence, and data for the other indoor microenvironments not specified in the model.

Management Considerations. The application of the SHEDS-PM model to the Philadelphia population gave insights into data needs and areas for model refinement. The continued development and evaluation of the SHEDS-PM population exposure model are being conducted as part of ORD's effort to develop a source-to-dose modeling system for PM and air toxics. This type of exposure and dose modeling system is considered to be important for the scientific and policy evaluation of the critical pathways, as well as the exposure factors and source types influencing human exposures to a variety of environmental pollutants, including PM.

Selected References. The results of the analysis were published in:

Burke, J., M. Zufall, and H. Özkaynak. 2001. "A Population Exposure Model for Particulate Matter: Case Study Results for $PM_{2.5}$ in Philadelphia, PA." *Journal of Exposure Analysis and Environmental Epidemiology* 11 (6): 470–89.

Georgepoulos, P. G., S. W. Wang, V. M. Vyas, Q. Sun, J. Burke, R. Vedantham, T. McCurdy, and H. Özkaynak. 2005. "A Source-to-Dose Assessment of Population Exposure to Fine PM and Ozone in Philadelphia, PA, During a Summer 1999 Episode." *Journal of Exposure Analysis and Environmental Epidemiology* 15 (5): 439–57.

Case Study 12: Probabilistic Analysis in Cumulative Risk Assessment of Organophosphorus Pesticides

In 1996, Congress enacted the Food Quality Protection Act (FQPA), which requires EPA to consider "available evidence concerning the cumulative effects on infants and children of such residues and other substances that have a common mechanism of toxicity" when setting pesticide tolerances (i.e., the maximum amount of pesticide residue legally allowed to remain on food products). FQPA also mandated that EPA completely reassess the safety of all existing pesticide tolerances (those in effect since August 1996) to ensure that they are supported by current scientific data and meet current safety standards. Because organophosphorus pesticides (OPs) were assigned priority for tolerance reassessment, these pesticides were the first "common mechanism" group identified by EPA's OPP. The ultimate goal associated with this cumulative risk assessment (CRA) was to provide a basis for the decision maker to establish safe tolerance levels for this group of pesticides, while meeting the FQPA standard for protecting infants and children.

Probabilistic Analysis. This case study provides an example of an advanced probabilistic assessment (Group 3). In 2006, EPA analyzed exposures to 30 OPs through food consumption, drinking water intake, and exposure via pesticide application. Distributions of human exposure factors, such as breathing rates, body weight and surface areas used in the assessment, came from the Agency's *Exposure Factors Handbook* (USEPA 1997d). EPA used Calendex, a probabilistic computer software program (available at http://www.epa.gov/pesticides/science/deem/) to integrate various pathways, while simultaneously incorporating the time dimensions of the input data. Based on the results of the exposure assessment, EPA calculated margins of exposure (MOEs) for the total cumulative risk from all pathways for each age group (infant less than 1; children 1–2, 3–5, 6–12; youth 13–19; and adults 20–49 and 50+ years of age).

The food component of the OPs CRA was highly refined, as it was based on residue monitoring data from the USDA's PDP and supplemented with information from the FDA's Surveillance Monitoring Programs and Total Diet Study. The residue data were combined with actual consumption data from USDA's Continuing Survey of Food Intakes by Individuals (CSFII) using probabilistic techniques. The CRA evaluated drinking water exposures on a regional basis. The assessment focused on areas where combined OP exposure is likely to be highest within each region. Primarily, the analysis used probabilistic modeling to estimate the co-occurrence of OP residues in water. Monitoring data were not available with enough consistency to be the sole basis for the assessment; however, they were used to corroborate the modeling results. Data sources for the water component of the assessment included USDA Agricultural Usage Reports for Field Crops, Fruits and Vegetables; USDA Typical Planting and Harvesting Dates for Field Crops and Fresh Market and Processing Vegetables; local sources for refinements; and monitoring studies from the U.S. Geological Survey (USGS) and other sources. Finally, exposure via the oral, dermal and inhalation routes resulting from applications of OPs in and around homes, schools, offices and other public areas were assessed probabilistically for each of the seven regions. The data sources for this part of the assessment included information from surveys and task forces, special studies and reports from published scientific literature, EPA's *Exposure Factors Handbook* (USEPA 1997d), and other sources.

Results of Analysis. The OPs CRA presented potential risk from single-day (acute) exposures across 1 year and from a series of 21-day rolling averages across the year. MOEs at the 99.9th percentile were approximately 100 or greater for all populations for the 21-day average results. The only exception is a brief period (roughly 2 weeks) in which drinking water exposures (identified from the *Exposure Factors Handbook*, USEPA 1997d) attributed to phorate use on sugarcane resulted in MOEs near 80 for children ages 1 to 2 years. Generally, exposures through the food pathway dominated total MOEs, and exposures through drinking water were substantially lower throughout most of the year. Residential exposures were substantially smaller than exposures through both food and drinking water.

The OPs CRA was very resource intensive. Work began in 1997 with the preparation of guidance documents and the development of a CRA methodology. Over 2 to 3 years, more than 25 people spent 50 to 100 percent of their time working on the assessment, with up to 50 people working on the CRA at critical periods. EPA has spent approximately $1 million on this assessment (e.g., for computers, models and contractor support).

Management Considerations. The OPs CRA was a landmark demonstration of the feasibility of a regulatory-level assessment of the risk from multiple chemicals. Upon completion, EPA presented the CRA at numerous public technical briefings and FIFRA SAP meetings, and made all of the data inputs available to the public. The OPP's substantial effort to communicate methodologies, approaches and results to the stakeholders aided in the success of the OPs CRA. The stakeholders expressed appreciation for the transparent nature of the OPs CRA and recognized the innovation and hard work that went into developing the assessments.

Selected References. The 2006 assessment and related documents are available at http://www.epa.gov/pesticides/cumulative/common_mech_groups.htm#op.

USEPA (U.S. Environmental Protection Agency). 1997d. *Exposure Factors Handbook.* Washington, D.C.: National Center for Environmental Assessment, USEPA. http://cfpub.epa.gov/ncea/cfm/recordisplay.cfm?deid=12464.

Case Study 13: Probabilistic Ecological Effects Risk Assessment Models for Evaluating Pesticide Use

As part of the process of developing and implementing a probabilistic approach for ERA, an illustrative case was completed in 1996. This case involved both DRA and PRA for the effects of a hypothetical chemical X (ChemX) on birds and aquatic species. Following the recommendations of the SAP and in response to issues raised by OPP risk managers, the Agency began an initiative to refine the ERA process for evaluating the effects of pesticides to terrestrial and aquatic species within the context of FIFRA, the main statutory authority for regulating pesticides at the federal level. The key goals and objectives of EPA's initiative were to:

❑ Incorporate probabilistic tools and methods to provide an estimate on the magnitude and probability of effects.

❑ Build on existing data requirements for registration.

❑ Utilize, wherever possible, existing databases and create new ones from existing data sources to minimize the need to generate additional data.

❑ Focus additional data requirements on reducing uncertainty in key areas.

After proposing a four-level risk assessment scheme, with higher levels reflecting more refined risk assessment techniques, the Agency developed pilot models for both terrestrial and aquatic species. Refined risk assessment models (Level II) then were developed and used in a generic chemical case study that was presented to the SAP in 2001.

Probabilistic Analysis. This case study describes an advanced probabilistic model for the ecological effects of pesticides (Group 3). The terrestrial Level II model (version 2.0) is a multimedia exposure/effects model that evaluates acute mortality levels in generic or specific avian species over a user-defined exposure window. The spatial scale is at the field level, which includes the field and surrounding area. Both areas are assumed to meet the habitat requirements for each species, and contamination of edge or adjacent habitat from drift is assumed to be zero. For each individual bird considered in a run of the Level II model, a random selection of values is made for the major exposure input parameters to estimate an external oral dose equivalent for that individual. The estimated dose equivalent is compared to a randomly assigned tolerance for the individual preselected from the dose-response distribution. If the dose is greater than the tolerance, the individual is scored "dead," if not, the individual is scored "not dead." After multiple iterations of individuals, a probability density function of percent mortality is generated.

From May 29 to 31, 1996, the Agency presented two ERA case studies to the SAP for review and comment. Although recognizing and generally reaffirming the utility of EPA's current deterministic assessment process, the SAP offered a number of suggestions for improvement. Foremost among their suggestions was a recommendation to move beyond the existing deterministic assessment approach by developing the tools and methodologies necessary to conduct a probabilistic assessment of effects. Such an assessment would estimate the magnitude and probability of the expected impact and define the level of certainty and variation involved in the estimate; risk managers within EPA's OPP also had requested this information in the past.

The aquatic Level II model is a two-dimensional Monte Carlo risk model consisting of three main components: (1) exposure, (2) effects and (3) risk. The exposure scenarios used at Level II are intended to provide estimates for vulnerable aquatic habitats across a wide range of geographical conditions under which a pesticide product is used. The Level II risk evaluation process yields estimates of likelihood and magnitude of effects for acute exposures. For the estimate of acute risks, a distribution of estimated exposure and a distribution of lethal effects are combined through a 2-D MCA to obtain a distribution of joint probability functions. For the estimate of chronic risks, a distribution of exposure concentrations is compared to a chronic measurement endpoint. The risk analysis for chronic effects provides information only on the probability that the chronic endpoint assessed will be exceeded, not on the magnitude of the chronic effect expected.

Results of Analysis. As part of the process of developing and implementing a probabilistic approach for ERA, a case study was completed. The case study involved both DRAs and PRAs for effects of ChemX on birds and aquatic species. The deterministic screen conducted on ChemX concluded qualitatively that it could pose a high risk to both freshwater fish and invertebrates and showed that PRA was warranted. Based on the probabilistic analysis, it was concluded that the use of ChemX was expected to infrequently result in significant freshwater fish mortalities but routinely result in reduced growth and other chronic effects in exposed fish. Substantial mortalities and chronic effects to sensitive aquatic invertebrates were predicted to occur routinely after peak exposures.

Management Considerations. In its review of the case study, the FIFRA SAP congratulated the Agency on the effort made to conduct PRA of pesticide effects in ecosystems. The panel commented that the approach had progressed greatly from earlier efforts, and that the intricacy of the models was surprisingly good, given the time interval in which the Agency had to complete the task.

Following the case study, EPA refined the models based on the SAP comments. In addition, the terrestrial Level II model was refined to include dermal and inhalation exposure.

Selected References. An overview of the models is available at
http://www.epa.gov/oppefed1/ecorisk/fifrasap/rra_exec_sum.htm#Terrestrial.

Case Study 14: Expert Elicitation of Concentration-Response Relationship Between Fine Particulate Matter Exposure and Mortality

In 2002, the NRC recommended that EPA improve its characterization of uncertainty in the benefits assessment for proposed regulations of air pollutants. NRC recommended that probability distributions for key sources of uncertainty be developed using available empirical data or through formal elicitation of expert judgments. A key component of EPA's approach for assessing potential health benefits associated with air quality regulations targeting emissions of $PM_{2.5}$ and its precursors is the effect of changes in ambient $PM_{2.5}$ levels on mortality. Avoided premature deaths constitute, on a monetary basis, between 85 and 95 percent of the monetized benefits reported in EPA's retrospective and prospective Section 812A benefit-cost analyses of the Clean Air Act (CAA; USEPA 1997e and 1999) and in Regulatory Impact Analysis (RIA) for rules such as the Heavy Duty Diesel Engine/Fuel Rule (USEPA 2000c) and the Non-Road Diesel Engine Rule (USEPA 2004). In response to the NRC recommendation, EPA conducted an expert elicitation evaluation of the concentration-response relationship between $PM_{2.5}$ exposure and mortality.

Probabilistic Analysis. This case study provides an example of the use of expert elicitation (Group 3) to derive probabilistic estimates of the uncertainty in one element of a cost-benefit analysis. Expert elicitation uses carefully structured interviews to elicit from each expert a best estimate of the true value for an outcome or variable of interest, as well as their uncertainty about the true value. This uncertainty is expressed as a subjective probabilistic distribution of values and reflects each expert's interpretation of theory and empirical evidence from relevant disciplines, as well as their beliefs about what is known and not known about the subject of the study. For the $PM_{2.5}$ expert elicitation, the process consisted of development of an elicitation protocol, selection of experts, development of a briefing book, conduct of elicitation interviews, the use of expert input prior to and following individual elicitation of judgments and the expert judgments themselves. The elicitation involved personal interviews with 12 health experts who had conducted research on the relationship between $PM_{2.5}$ exposures and mortality.

The main quantitative question asked each expert to provide a probabilistic distribution for the average expected decrease in U.S. annual, adult and all-cause mortality associated with a 1 $\mu g/m^3$ decrease in annual average $PM_{2.5}$ levels. When answering the main quantitative question, each expert was instructed to consider that the total mortality effect of a 1 $\mu g/m^3$ decrease in ambient annual average $PM_{2.5}$ may reflect reductions in both short-term peak and long-term average exposures to $PM_{2.5}$. Each expert was asked to aggregate the effects of both types of changes in their answers. The experts were given the option to integrate their judgments about the likelihood of a causal relationship or threshold in the concentration-response function into their own distributions or to provide a distribution "conditional on" one or both of these factors.

Results of Analysis. The project team developed the interview protocol between October 2004 and January 2006. Development of the protocol was informed by an April 2005 symposium held by the project team, where numerous health scientists and analysts provided feedback; detailed pretesting with independent EPA scientists in November 2005; and discussion with the participating experts at a pre-elicitation workshop in January 2006. The elicitation interviews were conducted between January and April 2006. Following the interviews, the experts reconvened for a post-elicitation workshop in June 2006, in which the project team anonymously shared the results of all experts with the group.

The median estimates for the $PM_{2.5}$ mortality relationship were generally similar to estimates derived from the two epidemiological studies most often used in benefits assessment. However, in almost all cases, the spread of the uncertainty distributions elicited from the experts exceeded the statistical uncertainty bounds reported by the most influential epidemiologic studies, suggesting that the expert elicitation process was successful in developing more comprehensive estimates of uncertainty for the $PM_{2.5}$ mortality relationship. The uncertainty distributions for $PM_{2.5}$ concentration-response resulting from the expert elicitation process were used in the RIA for the revised NAAQS standard for $PM_{2.5}$ (promulgated on September 21, 2006). Because the NAAQS are exclusively health-based standards, this RIA played no part in EPA's determination to revise the $PM_{2.5}$ NAAQS. Benefits estimates in the RIA were presented as ranges and included additional information on the quantified uncertainty distributions surrounding the points on the ranges, derived from both epidemiological studies and the expert elicitation results. OMB's review of the RIA was completed in March 2007.

Management Considerations. The NAAQS are exclusively health-based standards, so these analyses were not used in any manner by EPA in determining whether to revise the NAAQS for $PM_{2.5}$. Moreover, the request to engage in the expert elicitation did not come from the CASAC, the official peer review body for the NAAQS; a decision to conduct the analyses does not reflect CASAC advice that such analyses inform NAAQS determinations. The analyses addressed comments from the NRC that recommended that probability distributions for key sources of uncertainty be addressed. The analyses were used in EPA's retrospective and prospective Section 812A benefit-cost analyses of the CAA (USEPA 1997e and 1999) and in RIAs for rules such as the Heavy Duty Diesel Engine/Fuel Rule (USEPA 2000c) and the Non-Road Diesel Engine Rule (USEPA 2004). In response to the NRC recommendation, EPA conducted an expert elicitation evaluation of the concentration-response relationship between $PM_{2.5}$ exposure and mortality.

Selected Reference. The assessment is available at http://www.epa.gov/ttn/ecas/ria.html.

Case Study 15: Expert Elicitation of Sea-Level Rise Resulting From Global Climate Change

The United Nations Framework Convention on Climate Change requires nations to implement measures for adapting to rising sea level and other effects of changing climate. To decide on an appropriate response, coastal planners and engineers weigh the cost of these measures against the likely cost of failing to prepare, which depends on the probability of the sea rising a particular amount. The U.S. National Academy of Engineering recommended that assessments of sea level rise should provide probability estimates. Coastal engineers regularly employ probability information when designing structures for floods, and courts use probabilities to determine the value of land expropriated by regulations. This 1995 case study describes the development of a probability distribution for sea level rise, using models employed by previous assessments, as well as the expert opinions of 20 climate and glaciology reviewers about the probability distributions for particular model coefficients.

Probabilistic Analysis. This case study provides an example both of an analysis describing the probability of sea level rise, as well as an expert elicitation of the likelihood of particular models and probability distributions of the coefficients used by those models to predict future sea level rise (Group 3). The assessment of the probability of sea level rise used existing models describing the change in five components of sea level rise associated with greenhouse gas-related climate change (thermal expansion, small glaciers, polar precipitation, melting and ice discharge from Greenland

and ice discharge from Antarctica). To provide a starting point for the expert elicitation, initial probability distributions were assigned to each model coefficient based on the published literature.

After the initial probabilistic assessment was completed, the draft report was circulated to expert reviewers considered most qualified to render judgments on particular processes for revised estimates of the likelihood of particular models and the model coefficients' probability distributions. Experts representing both extremes of climate change science (those who predicted trivial consequences and those who predicted catastrophic effects; individuals whose thoughts had been excluded from previous assessments) were included. The experts were asked to provide subjective assessments of the probabilities of various models and model coefficients. These subjective probability estimates were used in place of the initial probabilities in the final model simulations. Different reviewer opinions were not combined to produce a single probability distribution for each parameter; instead, each reviewer's opinions were used in independent iterations of the simulation. The group of simulations resulted in the probability distribution of sea level rise.

Results of Analysis. The analysis, completed with a budget of $100,000, provided a probabilistic estimate of sea level rise for use by coastal engineers and regulators. The results suggested that there is a 65 percent chance that the sea level will rise 1 millimeter (mm) per year more rapidly in the next 30 years than it has been rising in the last century. Under the assumption that nonclimatic factors do not change, the projections suggested that there is a 50 percent chance that the global sea level will rise 45 centimeters (cm), and a 1 percent chance of a 112 cm rise by the year 2100. The median prediction of sea level rise was similar to the midpoint estimate of 48 cm published by the Intergovernmental Panel on Climate Change (IPCC) shortly thereafter (IPCC 1996). The report also found a 1 percent chance of a 4 to 5 meter rise over the next 2 centuries.

Management Considerations. There are two reports (USEPA 1995c; Titus and Narayanan 1996) that discuss several uses of the results of this study. By providing a probabilistic representation of sea level rise, the assessment allows coastal residents to make decisions with recognition of the uncertainty associated with predicted change. Rolling easements that vest when the sea rises to a particular level can be properly valued in both "arms-length" transaction sales or when calculating the allowable deduction for a charitable contribution of the easement to a conservancy. Cost-benefit assessments of alternative infrastructure designs—which already consider flood probabilities— also can consider sea level rise uncertainty. Assessments of the benefits of preventing an acceleration of sea level rise can include more readily low-probability outcomes, which can provide a better assessment of the true risk when the damage function is nonlinear, which often is the case.

Selected References.

USEPA (U.S. Environmental Protection Agency). 1995c. *The Probability of Sea Level Rise.* EPA/230/R-95/008. Washington, D.C.: Climate Change Division, USEPA. http://nepis.epa.gov/Exe/ZyPURL.cgi?Dockey=20011G1O.txt

IPCC (Intergovernmental Panel on Climate Change). 1996. *Climate Change 1995: The Science of Climate Change. Contribution of Working Group I to the Second Assessment of the Intergovernmental Panel on Climate Change.* Cambridge: Cambridge University Press.

Titus, J. G., and V. Narayanan. 1996. "The Risk of Sea Level Rise." *Climatic Change* 33(2): 151–212.

Case Study 16: Knowledge Elicitation for a Bayesian Belief Network Model of Stream Ecology

The identification of the causal pathways leading to stream impairment is a central challenge to understanding ecological relationships. Bayesian belief networks (BBNs) are a promising tool for modeling presumed causal relationships, providing a modeling structure within which different factors describing the ecosystem can be causally linked and calculating uncertainties expressed for each linkage.

BBNs can be used to model complex systems that involve several interdependent or interrelated variables. In general, a BBN is a model that evaluates situations where some information already is known, and incoming data are uncertain or partially unavailable. The information is depicted with influence diagrams that present a simple visual representation of a decision problem, for which quantitative estimates of effect probabilities are assigned. As such, BBNs have the potential for representing ecological knowledge and uncertainty in a format that is useful for predicting outcomes from management actions or for diagnosing the causes of observed conditions. Generally, specification of a BBN can be performed using available experimental data, literature review information (secondary data) and expert elicitation. Attempts to specify a BBN for the linkage between fine sediment load and macroinvertebrate populations using data from literature reviews have failed because of the absence of consistent conceptual models and the lack of quantitative data or summary statistics needed for the model. In light of these deficiencies, an effort was made to use expert elicitation to specify a BBN for the relationship between fine sediment load resulting from human activity and populations of macroinvertebrates. The goals of this effort were to examine whether BBNs might be useful for modeling stream impairment and to assess whether expert opinion could be elicited to make the BBN approach useful as a management tool.

Probabilistic Analysis. This case study provides an example of expert elicitation in the development of a BBN model of the effect of increased fine sediment load in a stream on macroinvertebrate populations (Group 3). For the purpose of this study, a stream setting (a Midwestern, low-gradient stream) and a scenario of impairment (introduction of excess fine sediment) were used. Five stream ecologists with experience in the specified geographic setting were invited to participate in an elicitation workshop. An initial model was depicted using influence diagrams, with the goals of structuring and specifying the model using expert elicitation. The ecologists were guided through a knowledge elicitation session in which they defined factors that described relevant chemical, physical and biological aspects of the ecosystem. The ecologists then described how these factors were connected and were asked to provide subjective, quantitative estimates of how different attributes of the macroinvertebrate assemblage would change in response to increased levels of fine sediment. Elicited input was used to restructure the model diagram and to develop probabilistic estimates of the relationships among the variables.

Results of Analysis. The elicited input was compiled and presented in terms of the model as structured by the stream ecologists and their model specifications. The results were presented both as revised influence diagrams and with Bayesian probabilistic terms representing the elicited input. The study yielded several important lessons. Among these were that the elicitation process takes time (including an initial session by teleconference as well as a 3-day workshop), defining a scenario with an appropriate degree of detail is critical and elicitation of complex ecological relationships is feasible.

Management Considerations. The study was considered successful for several reasons. First, the feasibility of the elicitation approach to building stream ecosystem models was demonstrated. The study also resulted in the development of new graphical techniques to perform the elicitation. The elicited input was interpreted in terms of predictive distributions to support fitting a complete Bayesian model. Furthermore, the study was successful in bringing together a group of experts in a particular subject area for the purpose of sharing information and learning about expert elicitation in support of model building. The exercise provided insights into how best to adapt knowledge elicitation methods to ecological questions and informed the assembled stream ecologists on the elicitation process and on the potential benefits of this modeling approach. The explicit quantification of uncertainty in the model not only enhances the utility of the model predictions, but also can help guide future research.

Selected References.

Black, P., T. Stockton, L. Yuan, D. Allan, W. Dodds, L. Johnson, M. Palmer, B. Wallace, and A. Stewart. 2005. "Using Knowledge Elicitation to Inform a Bayesian Belief Network Model of a Stream Ecosystem." *Eos, Transactions, American Geophysical Union* 86 (18), Joint Assembly Supplement, Abstract #NB41E-05.

Yuan, L. 2005. "TI: A Bayesian Approach for Combining Data Sets to Improve Estimates of Taxon Optima." *Eos, Transactions, American Geophysical Union* 86 (18), Joint Assembly Supplement, Abstract #NB41E-04.

CASE STUDY REFERENCES

Black, P., T. Stockton, L. Yuan, D. Allan, W. Dodds, L. Johnson, M. Palmer, B. Wallace, and A. Stewart. 2005. "Using Knowledge Elicitation to Inform a Bayesian Belief Network Model of a Stream Ecosystem." *Eos, Transactions, American Geophysical Union* 86 (18), Joint Assembly Supplement, Abstract #NB41E-05.

Burke, J., M. Zufall, and H. Özkaynak. 2001. "A Population Exposure Model for Particulate Matter: Case Study Results for $PM_{2.5}$ in Philadelphia, PA." *Journal of Exposure Analysis and Environmental Epidemiology* 11 (6): 470–89.

Connelly, N. A., T. L. Brown, and B. A. Knuth. 1990. *New York Statewide Angler Survey 1988.* Albany, NY: Bureau of Fisheries, New York Department of Environmental Conservation.

Georgepoulos, P. G., S. W. Wang, V. M. Vyas, Q. Sun, J. Burke, R. Vedantham, T. McCurdy, and H. Özkaynak. 2005. "A Source-to-Dose Assessment of Population Exposure to Fine PM and Ozone in Philadelphia, PA, During a Summer 1999 Episode." *Journal of Exposure Analysis and Environmental Epidemiology* 15 (5): 439–57.

IPCC (Intergovernmental Panel on Climate Change). 1996. *Climate Change 1995: The Science of Climate Change.* Contribution of Working Group I to the Second Assessment of the IPPC. Cambridge: Cambridge University Press.

Jamieson, D. 1996. "Scientific Uncertainty and the Political Process." *Annals of the American Academy of Political and Social Science* 545: 35–43.

Kurowicka, D., and R. Cooke. 2006. *Uncertainty Analysis With High Dimensional Dependent Modeling.* Wiley Series in Probability and Statistics. New York: John Wiley & Sons.

Langstaff, J. E. 2007. *Analysis of Uncertainty in Ozone Population Exposure Modeling.* Office of Air Quality Planning and Standards Staff Memorandum to Ozone NAAQS Review Docket. OAR-2005-0172. Washington, D.C.: USEPA. http://www.epa.gov/ttn/naaqs/standards/ozone/s_ozone_cr_td.html.

Olsen AR, Kincaid TM, Payton Q. 2012. Spatially balanced survey designs for natural resources. In: Gitzen RA, Millspaugh JJ, Cooper AB, Licht DS (eds) Design and Analysis of Long-Term Ecological Monitoring Studies. Cambridge University Press, Cambridge, UK, pp 126-150

Stahl, C. H., and A. J. Cimorelli. 2005. "How Much Uncertainty Is Too Much and How Do We Know? A Case Example of the Assessment of Ozone Monitor Network Options." *Risk Analysis* 25 (5): 1109–20.

Titus, J. G. and V. Narayanan. 1996. "The Risk of Sea Level Rise: A Delphic Monte Carlo Analysis in Which Twenty Researchers Specify Subjective Probability Distributions for Model Coefficients Within Their Respective Areas of Expertise." *Climatic Change* 33 (2): 151–212.

USEPA (U.S. Environmental Protection Agency). 1992a. *Guidelines for Exposure Assessment.* EPA/600/Z-92/001. Washington, D.C.: Risk Assessment Forum, USEPA. http://cfpub.epa.gov/ncea/cfm/recordisplay.cfm?deid=15263.

USEPA. 1992b. *Framework for Ecological Risk Assessment.* EPA/630/R-92/001. Washington, D.C.: Risk Assessment Forum, USEPA. http://www.epa.gov/raf/publications/framework-eco-risk-assessment.htm.

USEPA. 1995a. *Guidance for Risk Characterization.* Washington, D.C.: Science Policy Council, USEPA. http://www.epa.gov/spc/pdfs/rcguide.pdf.

USEPA. 1995b. *Policy on Evaluating Health Risks to Children.* Washington, D.C.: Science Policy Council, USEPA. http://www.epa.gov/spc/pdfs/memohlth.pdf.

USEPA. 1995c. *The Probability of Sea Level Rise.* EPA/230/R-95/008. Washington, D.C.: Office of Policy, Planning, and Evaluation, USEPA. http://nepis.epa.gov/Exe/ZyPURL.cgi?Dockey=20011G1O.txt.

USEPA. 1997a. *Policy for Use of Probabilistic Analysis in Risk Assessment at the U.S. Environmental Protection Agency.* Washington, D.C.: Science Policy Council, USEPA. http://www.epa.gov/spc/pdfs/probpol.pdf.

USEPA. 1997b. *Guiding Principles for Monte Carlo Analysis.* EPA/630/R-97/001. Washington, D.C.: Risk Assessment Forum, USEPA. http://www.epa.gov/raf/publications/pdfs/montecar.pdf.

USEPA. 1997c. *Guidance on Cumulative Risk Assessment. Part 1: Planning and Scoping.* Washington, D.C.: Science Policy Council, USEPA. http://www.epa.gov/spc/pdfs/cumrisk2.pdf.

USEPA. 1997d. *Exposure Factors Handbook.* Washington, D.C.: National Center for Environmental Assessment, USEPA. http://cfpub.epa.gov/ncea/cfm/recordisplay.cfm?deid=12464.

USEPA. 1997e. *Final Report to Congress on Benefits and Costs of the Clean Air Act, 1970 to 1990.* EPA/410/R-97/002. Cincinnati, OH: Office of Air and Radiation, USEPA.

USEPA. 1998. *Guidelines for Ecological Risk Assessment.* EPA/630/R-95/002F. Washington, D.C.: Risk Assessment Forum, USEPA. http://www.epa.gov/raf/publications/pdfs/ECOTXTBX.PDF.

USEPA. 1999. *The Benefits and Costs of the Clean Air Act 1990 to 2010: EPA Report to Congress.* EPA/410/R-99/001. Washington, D.C.: Office of Air and Radiation, USEPA. http://www.epa.gov/oar/sect812/1990-2010/chap1130.pdf.

USEPA. 2000a. *EPA Science Policy Council Handbook: Risk Characterization.* EPA/100/B-00/002. Washington, D.C.: Science Policy Council, USEPA. http://www.epa.gov/spc/pdfs/rchandbk.pdf.

USEPA. 2000b. *Phase 2 Report: Further Site Characterization and Analysis. Volume 2F—Revised Human Health Risk Assessment, Hudson River PCBs Reassessment RI/FS.* New York: Region 2, USEPA. http://www.epa.gov/hudson/revisedhhra-text.pdf.

USEPA. 2000c. *Final Heavy Duty Engine/Diesel Fuel Rule: Air Quality Estimation, Selected Health and Welfare Benefits Methods, and Benefit Analysis Results.* Research Triangle Park, NC: Office of Air Quality Planning and Standards, USEPA. http://www.epa.gov/ttnecas1/regdata/Benefits/tsdhddv8.pdf.

USEPA. 2001. *Risk Assessment Guidance for Superfund: Volume III — Part A, Process for Conducting Probabilistic Risk Assessment.* EPA/540/R-02/002. Washington, D.C.: Office of Emergency and Remedial Response, USEPA. http://www.epa.gov/oswer/riskassessment/rags3adt/pdf/rags3adt_complete.pdf.

USEPA. 2002. *EMAP Research Strategy.* EPA 620/R-02/002. Research Triangle Park, NC: Environmental Monitoring and Assessment Program, NHEERL, USEPA. http://www.epa.gov/nheerl/emap/files/emap_research_strategy.pdf.

USEPA. 2004. *An Examination of EPA Risk Assessment Principles and Practices.* EPA/100/B-04/001. Washington, D.C.: Office of the Science Advisor, USEPA. http://www.epa.gov/osa/pdfs/ratf-final.pdf.

USEPA. 2005. *Ozone Health Assessment Plan: Scope and Methods for Exposure Analysis and Risk Assessment.* Research Triangle Park, NC: Office of Air Quality Planning and Standards, USEPA. http://www.epa.gov/ttn/naaqs/standards/ozone/data/o3_health_assessment_plan_april05.pdf.

USEPA. 2006. *Total Risk Integrated Methodology (TRIM)—Air Pollutants Exposure Model Documentation (TRIM.Expo/APEX, Version 4) Volume I: User's Guide; Volume II: Technical Support Document.* Research Triangle Park, NC: Office of Air Quality Planning and Standards, USEPA. http://www.epa.gov/ttn/fera/human_apex.html.

USEPA. 2007a. *Review of National Ambient Air Quality Standards for Ozone: Policy Assessment of Scientific and Technical Information—OAQPS Staff Paper.* Research Triangle Park, NC: Office of Air Quality Planning and Standards, USEPA. http://www.epa.gov/ttn/naaqs/standards/ozone/data/2007_07_ozone_staff_paper.pdf.

USEPA. 2007b. *Ozone Population Exposure Analysis for Selected Urban Areas.* EPA/452/R-07-010. Research Triangle Park, NC: Office of Air Quality Planning and Standards, USEPA. http://www.epa.gov/ttn/naaqs/standards/ozone/data/2007_07_o3_exposure_tsd.pdf.

USEPA. 2014. *Framework for Human Health Risk Assessment to Inform Decision Making.* EPA/100/R-14/001. Washington, D.C.: Risk Assessment Forum, Office of the Science Advisor, USEPA. http://www.epa.gov/raf/frameworkhhra.htm

USGAO (U.S. Government Accountability Office). 2000. *Water Quality: Key EPA and State Decisions Limited by Inconsistent and Incomplete Data.* GAO/RCED-00-54. Washington, D.C.: USGAO. http://www.environmental-auditing.org/Portals/0/AuditFiles/useng00ar_ft_key_epa.pdf.

Xue, J., V. G. Zartarian, H. Özkaynak, W. Dang, G. Glen, L. Smith, and C. Stallings. 2006. "A Probabilistic Arsenic Exposure Assessment for Children Who Contact Chromated Copper Arsenate (CCA)-Treated Playsets and Decks, Part 2: Sensitivity and Uncertainty Analyses." *Risk Analysis* 26 (2): 533–41.

Yuan, L. 2005. "TI: A Bayesian Approach for Combining Data Sets to Improve Estimates of Taxon Optima." *Eos, Transactions, American Geophysical Union* 86 (18), Joint Assembly Supplement, Abstract #NB41E-04.

Zartarian, V. G., J. Xue, H. A. Özkaynak, W. Dang, G. Glen, L. Smith, and C. Stallings. 2006. *A Probabilistic Exposure Assessment for Children Who Contact CCA-Treated Playsets and Decks Using the Stochastic Human Exposure and Dose Simulation Model for the Wood Preservative Scenario (SHEDS-Wood), Final Report.* EPA/600/X-05/009. Washington, D.C.: USEPA.

Zartarian, V. G., J. Xue, H. A. Özkaynak, W. Dang, G. Glen, L. Smith, and C. Stallings. 2006. "A Probabilistic Arsenic Exposure Assessment for Children Who Contact Chromated Copper Arsenate (CAA)-Treated Playsets and Decks, Part 1: Model Methodology, Variability Results, and Model Evaluation." *Risk Analysis* 26 (2): 515–31.

Made in the USA
San Bernardino, CA
03 April 2018